"I am moved by what I have read. Such courage, honesty and common sense!"

Dr. DeRionne P. Pollard,
President, Montgomery College, Maryland

"An energized and supportive teacher can make the difference between an engaging lesson and a monotonous one. *The Heart of Education* contains all the necessary tools and strategies for teachers to rediscover this energy and encourage the same energy and excitement in their students. As a student myself, I believe that if every one of my teachers were to put into effect all the suggested practices in this book, both teachers and students would experience a renewed sense of purpose, productivity, and joy both in and out of the classroom."

Chopper Carter Schelp,
Sophomore Student, Walter Johnson High School, Maryland

"Dara's personal story and teaching experiences help us remember the importance of some of the intangible aspects of teaching. It's a valuable lesson."

Dr. Donna Wiseman,
Dean, University of Maryland College of Education

"As the debate about character education in the UK and around the world intensifies, we must heed *The Heart of Education*, a narrative that pulses with unmatched experience and inspirational advice. An essential purchase."

Geoff Smith,
Headteacher, Kehelland School, Cornwall, UK

"I am so proud to have had Dara Feldman as my fourth grade teacher and I am pleased that others will 'hear' her message through this book. It was because of her passion for teaching and her love for her students that I became a teacher myself. I wonder how many of her students became teachers as well? A good chunk of us, I'm sure! I am no longer teaching in a classroom but am staying home to raise my children. I've started applying what I read in *The Heart of Education* to how I raise my children and the results are inspiring! This is a go-to manual for both teachers and parents."

Sonia Reed Smith,
Mother, Wife & Teacher

"Dara Feldman is a powerful force for good. She is determined to help all of us make our world a better place, and her book can help us do just that."

Jim Knight,
Researcher & Author, *Unmistakable Impact*

"The Virtues Project is such a valuable tool for supporting the classroom climate and well-being of students and teachers that I wish I had known about it when I was a teacher! I hope this book will be a jumping-off point for readers to incorporate Virtues language and practices into their personal lives, communities and schools."

Camille Whitney,
Education PhD Candidate, Stanford University

The Heart of Education

Bringing Joy, Meaning and Purpose
Back to Teaching and Learning

by Dara Feldman

M⊙tivationalPRESS®
LEADERS IN GLOBAL PUBLISHING

Published by Motivational Press, Inc.
7777 N Wickham Rd, # 12-247
Melbourne, FL 32940
www.MotivationalPress.com

Manufactured in the United States of America.

ISBN: 978-1-62865-069-3

Dedication

*To Dave, my loving and supportive husband,
whose encouragement lifts me up daily.*

*To Dani and Jake, my courageous and compassionate children,
whose idealism gives me faith in the future of humanity.*

*To my Dad, whose unconditional love and acceptance gives me
the courage and strength to be my own person.*

*To my Mom, whose perseverance and independence
inspires me to chart my own course.*

*To Devin, my brother, whose generosity and
guidance propels me forward.*

*To Mrs. O'Leary, my 3rd grade teacher, whose compassion and
caring is the reason I became a teacher.*

*To all of my students, past, present and future, who inspire me to
bring joy, meaning and purpose back to teaching and learning.*

Contents

Foreword

"Our job is not to figure out the 'how.'
The 'how' will show up out of the commitment and
belief in the 'what.'"

Jack Canfield

Having been a public school teacher on the south side of Chicago, I know first hand the challenges educators face on a daily basis. "Overcoming negative self-concept is one of the most prevalent problems facing all educators today—kindergarten through college. Students of all ages seem to be suffering from not liking themselves." I wrote these words in 1986 when I authored *Self Esteem in the Classroom: A Curriculum Guide.* Though the book is more than 25 years old, I believe the problem is even greater today.

Over the past decade we have been so focused on academics and competition that our children often feel that they have been reduced to a number, a statistic, be it a test score or an IQ. Even five year olds are beginning to feel unworthy at a young age if they cannot read at a certain level by the end of kindergarten. This lack of authentic self-esteem shows up in a variety of ways. Students do not have the confidence and determination to do their personal best when confronted with challenges. They may perform poorly in school, chronically skip class or drop out of school all together which can often result in them ending up on the streets, in prison or even worse in the morgue. When students suffer from low self-esteem and poor social and emotional skills they may have a hard time making and keeping friends and therefore feel isolated, rejected and alone. When these negative feelings arise, students can become depressed and suicidal turning their anger inward, or become aggressive and violent, turning their anger outward and harming others by bullying or even killing their fellow students.

There is hope, however. There are educators everywhere who have come to realize that low self-esteem can be overcome by intentionally teaching lessons on self-awareness, values, character, communication skills, and as Dara Feldman so brilliantly teaches us in this book, on virtues—the essential qualities of the heart. In *The Heart of Education*, Dara shares specific strategies to empower educators to know their own inherent value and help their students realize their potential as well. The book is both practical and inspiring because she shares her own personal stories and the stories of others as well as practical classroom strategies backed up by lots of research.

I am optimistic about the future of education because we now have unlimited access to new information about topics such as brain research, positive psychology, social emotional learning, character development, motivation and quantum physics. What used to be considered far out or "woowoo" has now become more mainstream as it is backed up by science and research.

In 1986, when Dara was in her second year of teaching and working at a challenging urban school outside of Washington, DC, she bought my book, *Self Esteem in the Classroom*, and began using the concepts with her students, thus beginning her journey of transformation. Over the years she has internalized my *Success Principles* and used what she has learned as stepping stones to guide her along the path to where she is today. In 2009, Dara was honored as Teacher of the Year for the National Association for Self Esteem, an association that I co-founded. Now Dara's commitment is to help other educators remember that they also have the ability to co-create their destinies and to empower their students to do the same. I trust that this book will open your heart and reawaken your spirit as you read it and that you will be inspired into action. Our kids need you.

I wish you a life—both in and outside the classroom filled with love, joy, meaning, purpose and fulfillment.

With love and appreciation for who you are and all you do as an educator...

Jack Canfield
Co-creator of the Chicken Soup for the Soul® series

Wake Up Everybody

by Harold Melvin and the Blue Notes

"Wake up all the teachers time to teach a new way

Maybe then they'll listen to whatcha have to say

Cause they're the ones who's coming up and the world is in their hands

When you teach the children teach 'em the very best you can

The world won't get no better if we just let it be

The world won't get no better we gotta change it yeah, just you and me."

Introduction

"For me, the greatest contribution you can make to the world
is to grow in self-awareness, self-realization, and the power to
manifest your own heartfelt dreams and desires.
The second greatest thing you can do is to help others do the same."
Jack Canfield

In June of 2006, as a result of being honored as Disney's Outstanding Elementary Teacher of the Year, I left the classroom and the school system I loved to share what I had learned about bringing joy, meaning and purpose back to teaching and learning. That is the purpose of this book.

For several years leading up to my departure, I was becoming more and more disillusioned by what was and was not happening in education. Like so many other educators, I had gone into teaching to make a difference in the lives of children, and yet, now it felt as if all I was doing was pushing these kids as hard and as fast as possible. As my instructional coaching mentor, Jim Knight, wrote in his book, *Unmistakable Impact*, "When we take the humanity out of professional learning, we ignore the complexity of any helping relationship, and we make it almost impossible for learning to occur."

With all the focus on NCLB, AYP, SAT and AP, where was the L-O-V-E? Love for our students, love for our vocation and the love of learning itself. It didn't seem to matter what all of the research suggested about what was most important with regard to learning and helping children grow up to be happy, healthy, productive world citizens. Remember the three Rs of relationships, relevance and rigor? Well, we had pretty much kissed the first two Rs goodbye.

Receiving the Disney honor put me on the path which led me to The Virtues Project. I knew I had found something revolutionary, and I immediately started utilizing The Five Strategies of the project in my classroom.

The Five Strategies of The Virtues Project™, outlined below, inspire individuals to live more authentic, joyful lives, families to raise children of compassion and integrity, educators to create safe, caring and high performing learning communities, and leaders to inspire excellence and ethics in the workplace.

1. Speak the Language of Virtues: Language has the power to inspire or to discourage. Using virtues to acknowledge, guide, correct and thank awakens the best within us.
2. Recognize Teachable Moments: Recognizing the virtues needed in daily challenges helps us to become lifelong learners open to the lessons of character.
3. Set Clear Boundaries: Boundaries based on respect and restorative justice create a climate of peace, cooperation and safety in our homes, schools and communities.
4. Honor the Spirit: We sustain our vision and purpose by integrating virtues into our activities, surroundings, celebrations and the arts.
5. Offer Companioning: Being deeply present and listening with compassionate curiosity guides others to find clarity and to create their own solutions.

As I worked these strategies into my daily classroom activities, joy, meaning and purpose were quickly restored. I knew I had to share these strategies with other educators.

My hope is that this book will empower veteran educators to remember why they first went into teaching. In addition, I want to help up-and-coming educators maintain their idealism and commitment to this valuable profession by learning simple and powerful strategies for creating peaceful, joyful and high performing learning communities.

In the first three chapters I share my personal journey of transformation. Perhaps you will see yourself and/or your students somewhere in my story. Many of us have gone into education because of the love and support of a teacher who has made a difference in our lives. Some have become teachers in response to a painful experience that they want to protect others from experiencing. Having experienced my share of challenges, I have come out on the other side a more grateful and stronger person. The experience, strength and hope I write about will hopefully inspire you to set your own intentions and not only live inside your dreams, but use the skills and strategies shared in this book to make them a reality for yourself. Additionally, my wish is that you will see yourself, your colleagues, the families you work with and your students through a more loving and compassionate lens.

Chapter Four is focused on the importance of character education and social emotional learning. In Paul Tough's book *How Children Succeed: Grit, Curiosity and the Hidden Power of Character* he writes, "Character matters. There is no antipoverty tool we can provide for disadvantaged young people that will be more valuable than the character strengths... conscientiousness, grit, resilience, perseverance and optimism." He goes on to say that "Science suggests that the character strengths that matter so much to young people's success are not innate: they don't appear in us magically, as a result of good luck or good genes. And they are simply not a choice. They are rooted in brain chemistry, and they are molded, in measurable and predictable ways by the environment in which children grow up... We now know a great deal about what kind of interventions will help children develop those strengths and skills, starting at birth and going all the way through college." The rest of this book is about those interventions.

Chapters Five through Nine outline The Virtues Project's Five Strategies, powerful interventions to bring out the best in our students and ourselves. Each chapter explores one of The Five Strategies and has stories, examples, activities and research woven throughout to help you deepen in your understanding of each strategy.

Chapter Ten contains powerful examples of how The Virtues Project is transforming teaching and learning around the world.

I invite you to use this book as a valuable resource on your journey of personal and professional transformation. Personally, I hope that you open yourself to the possibilities of what The Virtues Project can bring to your life. Professionally, may your classroom community become an even more nurturing center that teaches how to learn and live in a world with love, respect and compassion.

With much caring and enthusiasm,
Dara Feldman
January 2013

Chapter One

A Journey of Transformation

"The meaning of life is to find your gift.
The purpose of life is to give it away."

Joy J. Golliver

My Inspiration

I am one of the lucky ones. I knew I wanted to be a teacher ever since I was eight years old and a student in Mrs. O'Leary's third grade class. An exceptional teacher, Mrs. O'Leary did not treat her students as mere "vessels to be filled" with reading, writing and arithmetic, but as individuals worthy of her time, respect and love. She always made me feel as if she had nothing but time for me, that I was a person with value, that I *mattered*. Having Mrs. O'Leary that year was just short of a miracle for me. It was an incredibly difficult year as I struggled with overwhelming challenges. At home, my mom was struggling with her second bout of breast cancer while also working on her doctorate. Additionally, although I did not know it at the time, she was in the beginning stages of alcoholism. Needless to say, she was not very available.

Around this time I was beginning my own devastating journey into compulsive overeating. Three years earlier I had been sexually abused by a babysitter. Like many victims, I kept silent and allowed the traumatic events of that horrifying day to take on an almost dream-like quality of unreality. What I could not escape, however, were the very real feelings of guilt and shame, and the sense that I was somehow at fault. I began eating constantly in an effort to stuff down those feelings, and perhaps, on some level, create a physical barrier with my weight so nothing like that could ever happen to me again. By the time I was in third grade, the effects of my eating were starting to show up not only as extra weight on my short body, but also in my behavior. I would sneak into the coat closet at school and steal food from my classmates' lunch boxes. I would sneak back into an empty classroom to steal change from their desks so I could buy ice cream at lunch to numb the pain and loneliness I felt. As I grew chubbier and chubbier, I became a target to many of my classmates who would tease and taunt me, and call me hurtful names like "Bahama Mama."

I didn't want to go out to recess because I knew I would get bullied. Mrs. O'Leary showed great compassion and understanding toward me and allowed me to stay in during recess to help her. I graded papers, made learning centers and created bulletin boards. I found that I genuinely loved it and her! She not only provided me with a safe harbor, she introduced me to two things that were to become my life's passion: education and the desire to help others know their inherent value.

I will be forever grateful to Mrs. O'Leary for loving me at a time when I felt unlovable, and showing me the importance of developing authentic relationships with students. As educators, we may never know when we are that ONE person who makes a difference in a student's life. Though I still had several difficult years ahead of me, Mrs. O'Leary helped lay the foundation for my path to a healthy, productive and spiritual life.

Fortunately, I have been able to let Mrs. O'Leary know how much she means to me. When she herself was nominated for the Disney Teacher Awards, I was the former student she honored with the opportunity to write her letter of recommendation. I was also privileged to be her teacher 30 years after she was mine when I was working as an instructional technology specialist teaching teachers how to use technology.

As I write this book, Mrs. O'Leary has started her 42nd year as a teacher and she claims it is her last. I see her influence extend to the next generation of teachers as my own daughter Dani, a recent graduate from the University of Maryland, begins her career in education, teaching social justice and dance with an organization called Dance4Peace. I am also thrilled to say that I have returned to Montgomery County Public Schools (MCPS) in Maryland for my fourth "tour of duty" working as a character development coach at Greencastle Elementary School (ES). How fortunate I am to be able to do the work I do around the world *here,* in my home school district, and in a school where I taught third grade 20 years ago!

History Chooses You

In Margaret J. Wheatley's essay "History Chooses You," from her book *Perseverance,* she writes, "We are both blessed and cursed when history chooses us. But once chosen we can't not do it." I knew exactly what she meant.

In 2005, while teaching kindergarten at Garrett Park Elementary School in MCPS, Maryland, I was selected as Disney's Outstanding Elementary Teacher of the Year. I believe that honor came, not because I am a better teacher than anyone else, but because I have a big mouth and a passion for justice that doesn't let me stop until the mission is accomplished. I know that I stand on the shoulders of amazing educators who I have worked with and learned from over the years, including Coach John Wooden, Jack Canfield, Linda Kavelin-Popov, Fred Rogers, John Dewey and many others. Their lessons and my passion have led me to become, in the words of Ms. Wheatley, "an accidental activist."

Be Careful What You Wish For

Not long after I learned I had been selected as a Disney Teacher, my husband Dave and I went to New York City to participate in a Peak Potentials Personal Development seminar called "The Millionaire Mind Intensive" (MMI), which had been suggested to me by a spiritual advisor I was working with. I really had no idea what the seminar was about, but since I trusted my advisor I was willing to attend.

While driving to New York, *I was thinking about the fact that we often teach what we most need to learn ourselves.* I wondered. *I know my ABCs, so I don't need to learn how to read. I can count to 31, so I've got the math thing going on.* And then it hit me: the big "Aha" moment, the 1000-watt light bulb illuminating the answer: *self-esteem.* The reason I went into education was to help students develop their self-esteem, to know and embrace their own dignity, and to reach their highest potential. I recognized that by doing this for them, I was doing it for myself as well. At that moment I wondered how this seminar was going to impact my mission, and I told my husband that if it was going to be all about money (after all, it *was* called the *Millionaire* Mind Intensive) then I was not going to participate!

As we walked up to the Millennium Hotel in New York City, I feared the participants would be focused solely on how to make money, and that the spiritual element I was craving would be absent. But as we opened the doors of the seminar we were greeted by 1,000 of what I soon recognized as some of the most spiritual people I had ever met!

During the seminar, we went through a variety of exercises where I began to understand some of my blocks, fears, and prejudices around money, and honestly, about people who have money. It really touched my husband and me at the core of our worthiness issues.

On the last day of MMI we were asked to set an intention. At that time, I had no idea of what an intention was or how to set one. We were told that an intention needs to be clear, time bound and written in the affirmative. Feeling a little skeptical about what we were doing, but determined to go along, I created the following intention: "I work with masters in education and spirituality to create a new educational paradigm… one where joy, meaning, purpose and peace are at the heart and I leverage the power of technology to do so." Though I did not know how on earth it would all happen, as I wrote my intention I did know it was truly a strong desire of my heart. I was committed to doing whatever it would take within my power to make it happen.

A Bridge Between Traditional Education and Spirituality

I am grateful to live in a time when more and more people recognize the value of incorporating spiritual beliefs and practices into their everyday lives. I feel we are gradually coming to a place where spirituality is not viewed as something practiced by religious fanatics or addled hippies, but that spirituality is something that can be defined and expressed by each one of us. It is about joy, meaning and purpose in one's own life. I believe I am a bridge between traditional education and spirituality, and that my life's purpose is to help other educators and students understand that they are co-creators of their destiny... what we think, say and do helps to shape our reality.

Around the same time that Dave and I participated in MMI, we heard about the movie "The Secret" which introduced us to the concept of "The Law of Attraction." The film explains The Law of Attraction as, "feelings and thoughts can attract events, feelings, and experiences, from the workings of the cosmos to interactions among individuals in their physical, emotional, and professional affairs." At first I was a bit skeptical but then I started realizing how The Law of Attraction had already worked in my life, and the lives of those around me, in many ways. I also came to understand that in some respects this was just another term for a "self-fulfilling prophecy."

Self-fulfilling prophecy, a term coined by 20th century sociologist Robert Merton, appears for the first time in his book *Social Theory and Social Structure*, published in 1949. In it he explains the prophecy or prediction is false but is made true by a person's actions. In the modern sense the prophecy has neither false nor true value, but is merely a possibility that is made into probability by a person's unconscious or conscious actions.

Growing up, my mom had always said, "Just shoot me if something happens to my brain. " My mother is a brilliant woman who spoke all around the world on the mental aspects of breast cancer. She was a true pioneer in women's health, especially with regard to the psychosocial aspects of breast cancer, reconstructive surgery and how this type of cancer affects intimacy and what can be done about it. My mother has many gifts and talents, but has always prized her intellectual abilities above all.

Then at age 56 my mom suffered a massive stroke, and she lay bleeding in her apartment in Long Beach, CA -- 3,000 miles away from my brother and me -- for more than two days, before she was found by a neighbor. She could not move or speak. It took her more than a decade to learn how to speak, walk, and remember, and many of the other ordinary daily activities we all take for granted. It also took her that long to finally accept that she would never work or drive again.

I often wondered if even the smallest part of what she experienced was the self-fulfilling prophecy of focusing on the negative. I then imagined what could happen instead if she, and all of us, focused on positive possibilities and how those thoughts might result in the highest and greatest good of all? I am relieved to say that 17 years after her stroke my mom is 73 years of age, and is actually once again enjoying her life.

OK, back to my intention. So armed with a powerful "pie in the sky" intention (or so I thought), in the fall of 2005 I began my 16th year as a classroom teacher. As a foundation for a positive classroom climate, my students and I used Coach John Wooden's book *Inch and Miles*. (For those of you who don't follow basketball, Wooden is one of the most revered and loved coaches of all times, bringing his UCLA basketball team to win 10 national championships in 12 years. He is also known for his inspirational messages to his players as well as his books on leadership.) *Inch and Miles* outlines Wooden's Success Pyramid for kids. Each morning my students and I chanted affirmations bringing to life the qualities Coach described as fundamental to success. Throughout the day we looked for and acknowledged the positive qualities we saw in one another.

We also played the song, "I'm A Person" (www.iamaperson. com) by David Giller. Giller, an amazingly creative master in spirituality who, along with his wildly creative and committed partner, Helene Abrams, has been on a lifelong quest to strengthen communities and provide cohesive frameworks and materials which promote positive life skills and healthy choices.

Singing this song every morning raised the energy level in our classroom and allowed us to start everyday in a joyful manner.

Taking part in these activities definitely helped start the year off on a positive note, and I was feeling pretty good about the climate in my classroom. However, I still felt there was something missing, and I couldn't quite figure out what it was.

The Boat Ride That Changed My Life Forever

In October of 2005, I returned once again to Disney for the professional development week with all the teachers who were honored that year by Disney. It was during those five days that I had the opportunity to spend some one-on-one time with David Vixie, the overall Disney Teacher of the Year. We were in a boat on one of the Disney rides and I asked him, "David, what in your repertoire speaks to you the most?" He pulled out a little card with a list of virtues and a website. I gasped aloud, and it was at that moment that I knew why I had received the Disney honor. Every word written on that card resonated to the very core of who I was as a teacher, and these words were what I wanted for each of my students. It was the very reason I went into education.

After the boat ride ended, I immediately went back to my hotel room, went onto the website (www.virtuesproject.org) and ordered almost all of The Virtues Project materials except a book called *A Pace of Grace*. At the time I did not see how *A Pace of Grace* could help me strengthen my own virtues and those of my students. Besides, it was the virtues that attracted me to the project.

When I returned to Maryland the following week, I got a phone call from Lisa, an acquaintance I knew from Overeaters Anonymous (OA), a 12 Step program which has given me freedom from compulsive overeating, bulimia and anorexia one day at a time for almost 20 years. Although we were friendly, we had never gotten together socially or talked very much on the phone. She told me she had just returned from California and had a present for me, which she would bring to the next meeting.

That Wednesday morning, when I met Lisa in the gravel parking lot of a local church, she had a brown paper bag in her hand. She reached in and pulled out a yellow paperback book, and I gasped for the second time in less than a week. She handed me a copy of *A Pace of Grace* by Linda Kavelin-Popov, thus completing my entire Virtues Project International (VPI) library. In the same week I had been introduced to The Virtues Project (VP) in Florida, Lisa had learned about the other side of VPI's work, *A Pace of Grace*, in California. Coincidence? I think not! I believe it was divinely inspired. Needless to say, Lisa is now one of my closest friends.

"Losing Amnesia" or the Gift of Remembering

Once my materials came and I had the chance to read *The Virtues Project Educator's Guide*, I began using The Five Strategies in my kindergarten class. Joy, meaning and purpose were restored once again. I lost the "No Child Left Behind" (NCLB) amnesia, that forgetfulness which can infect even the most inspired teachers when the joys of teaching are lost to "one size fits all" mandates of academic rigor and testing. As a result of the spiritual transformation I had experienced and the sense of self worth I discovered, now I had Five Strategies I could incorporate into my daily life and share with others. The transformative results were inspiring. No longer did I get Sunday anxiety pangs from the fear of possible power struggles or classroom management encounters I might not be able to work out in a peaceful or productive manner. I was now equipped with The Five Strategies of The Virtues Project and I had the confidence and the tools to create a peaceful classroom and empower my students to thrive. It was an awesome feeling.

Oftentimes as educators, we participate in professional development that can only be used at school or isn't relevant to the content or age level of students with whom we work. What makes The Virtues Project unique is that it is personal, professional and organizational development all rolled into one and it can be used at home, school and beyond. It is not an add-on curriculum. There is no "white binder." It is Five Strategies that can be used to enhance all areas of life.

The Instruction Manual Our Kids Didn't Come With

Now that I was using the tools of The Virtues Project, life at school with my kindergarteners was wonder-FULL. However, after school I would walk in the front door of my house and start raging at my 12 and 15-year-old! Sibling rivalry was at an all-time high, the house was a mess, and there was not a lot of respect being shown to one another.

It was during a fit of frustration, bordering on rage, that I remembered what happened when Linda, one of the founders of The Virtues Project, appeared on Oprah. Oprah said of *The Family Virtues Guide*, "Parents are always saying children don't come with a guide book, this is one. This helps you get them on the right track for leading a good life." (I don't know about you, but my children didn't come with an instruction manual.) So holding *The Family Virtues Guide* in one hand and a set of Virtues Project Educators Cards in the other, I was now armed with instructions for raising my children. I called a family meeting

Solutions over Supper

The four of us sat at the dining room table: my 12-year-old son Jake, my 15-year-old daughter Dani, my husband and me. I turned to page 31 of *The Family Guide*, which was the chapter on how to set family ground rules, and then asked my kids if they wanted to read the few pages or did they want me to read them. As expected, they said, "You do it." So I did.

After I finished reading from the guide, I took the Educators Cards and spread them across the table. I invited each person to pick a virtue they wanted to bring into our family. My daughter picked "Respect," my son picked "Flexibility" (no doubt because he was always trying to talk his way out of things!), my husband picked "Responsibility" and I picked "Orderliness."

We each read our card aloud and then we chose one to put through the process of using a virtue as a ground rule. We agreed on Respect. The first thing we did was make a list of what we wanted respect to look like in our home. For example, when you knock on the door wait for someone to say, "Come in" (so you don't accidentally walk in on your stepdaughter getting dressed). If you borrow something, give it back when you are done. If you are talking to someone, give him or her your full attention (do not multitask on the computer, iPad or iPhone). Use kind language and tone even when you are upset.

Next, we discussed the consequences. If you do not return something you borrowed, you may lose that privilege in the future. If you are multitasking while talking, the electronics get turned off or taken away for a period of time. If you choose not to use a respectful tone or language, you go to your room until you can get into a peaceful place, make amends and ask for what you need in a respectful way.

After we listed our ground rules and consequences, I gave everyone a piece of fluorescent lime green paper and asked each family member to fold it into quarters, put their name in the center and write one of our core family virtues at the top of each box. My fiery 15-year-old redhead put her hand on her hip, cocked her head and said, "Great, so now when we are not doing the virtue you are going to write it down!" I gently responded, "No. When I see you exhibiting a virtue I am going to give you a virtues acknowledgement." And with that, Dani's whole body relaxed and she responded with a relieved, "Oh."

Up on the refrigerator went the four virtues cards and four pieces of lime green paper. True to my word, I started looking for everyone's virtues. The results were surprisingly immediate. I walked into the powder room and the towel was on the towel rack instead of the floor. So I wrote on Jake's paper in the orderliness box, "Thank you for your orderliness hanging up the towel on the towel rack." I have learned that when giving a *virtues acknowledgment* to be very deliberate in my choice of words. If I had just put "thank you for your orderliness," Jake would not have known that hanging things up is orderly. And if I had just written "thank you for hanging up the towel on the towel rack," he may not have known that hanging things up is the virtue of orderliness. By naming the virtue and the evidence, it helps us internalize the virtues so that they become a transferable skill. Got it?

One night Dani joined us at dinner instead of going out with her friends. On her sheet under flexibility I wrote, "Dani, I honor your flexibility by having dinner with us instead of going out with your friends." Again you can see the pattern here with the language. There is an opening phrase of the sentence (the stem), the virtue, and the evidence that shows how that virtue was demonstrated.

The next morning I woke up to find an acknowledgement written from my daughter Dani. Under "respect" she wrote, "Mommy, thank you for showing respect by taking the time to write acknowledgements on our sheets." In less than 36 hours, identifying and acknowledging our family's core virtues had already made a significant impact on my children.

A Request Not to be Believed

Fast forward two years after our "Solutions over Supper" family meeting: my daughter, who was the captain of the Poms squad (dance team) at her high school, called to tell me their coach had quit at the beginning of the season. After she told me what had happened, she then actually asked me if I would be their coach! I almost passed out at her request. Who wants their mommy around every day after school for six months, especially when they are a graduating senior, right?

Fortunately, I had already developed a relationship with the 20 girls on the squad. Just a few weeks before my daughter's shocking request, the girls had a slumber party at our home (or as I call it, a-stay-up-all-night party, because no one ever sleeps!). At that party we did some team building. There were seven seniors on the squad, so I gave each senior a pack of Virtues Cards and invited them to get two other younger poms and select five to seven virtues they wanted to focus on this year as a squad.

Once the groups of three were done selecting, I had them "pair and share" with other groups, and then finally come together as a whole squad and form a consensus. The seven virtues they selected were: excellence, commitment, cooperation, enthusiasm, confidence, unity and love. Now as their coach I would play an active role in guiding these girls with the virtues they selected. These were the core virtues that we lived by throughout the entire season and they made a huge impact.

Before every practice, every game and every competition, the girls would circle up with lots of spirit and chant their virtues. If their energy was low during practice, the captains invited the girls to enthusiasm by saying something like, "Dancing is what we love, show your enthusiasm with big smiles, lots of bounce and high energy! That's it! Now I feel the joy!" If they were not performing moves as sharply as they could, we focused on excellence by saying, "Let's move with excellence and sharpen our moves, fully extend your arms and be mindful of your space."

The girls invested a lot of time practicing on their own and they were acknowledged for their commitment. Focusing on our core virtues made the six months we worked together incredibly joyful and meaningful, and created the climate for them to thrive.

Around the middle of January the girls started getting a bit short and catty with one another. (Not only is January competition season, it is also finals week. Who makes that crazy, stressful schedule anyway?) One of the seniors, who at the beginning of the season was the most skeptical about the virtues, asked that we call a "unity circle." I agreed and encouraged her to lead it. She invited the squad to sit in a circle so everyone could see each other. Then she read the unity card aloud and asked each girl to go around the circle and share what was on her mind and heart. They had to use "I statements" with no crosstalk. Each girl shared from her heart.

We went around the circle a couple of times and by the end of that process, peace and harmony had been restored. The girls went on to win every medal and trophy you could possibly win that year... 1st place, 2nd place, Spirit, Choreography and Best Captain... yet that was never their focus. They were committed to working in unity, with enthusiasm, confidence, excellence, creativity and love. Once again I had the privilege to witness in amazement what happens when the focus is on the virtues; the outcomes take care of themselves.

At the end of the second season, I was really touched when the girls presented me with the gift of a Voice Quilt. They all recorded special messages to me and then presented it to me on a CD.

Our junior captain's words epitomized the power of The Virtues Project for me: "I just wanted to say thank you for being our coach this year. I know in the summer, a few girls were skeptical about virtues, but now they are a vital part of our practice and they have definitely been a huge part of our success in competition this year. We have improved not only as poms but also in our attitudes. We are committed, we have confidence and unity. I can definitely say, not just for myself but for all the other girls, that these are the things that really make us winners."

What a gift to be able to experience the power of The Virtues Project as a kindergarten teacher, wife, mother and as a coach!

Idealism

Idealism is having a vision of what is possible and wanting to make a difference. It is caring passionately about what is meaningful in life. Idealists see things as they could be and have faith in the power of change. We put our principles into practice. We don't just accept the way things are. We dare to have big dreams and then act as if they are possible. Idealism doesn't mean that we are idle dreamers. Idle dreamers just wish things were better. Idealists do something to make things better. We make the ideal real.

The Virtues Project™

1 What made you want to become a teacher and how old were you when you knew?
2 Who are your mentors, your guides, and the people you look up to for inspiration?
3 What is it about them that inspires you?

Chapter Two

Sole Purpose or Soul Purpose

"Go confidently in the direction of your dreams!
Live the life you've imagined."
Henry David Thoreau

I would have been very happy teaching kindergarten for the rest of my career. It was such joyful and meaningful work, though I have to admit that it was getting harder and harder to "walk the talk." In the era of No Child Left Behind, it felt as if the "sole" purpose of public school education was to focus on academic rigor and testing. It felt to me as if we were losing what I believe is our "soul" purpose as educators: to help our students (and one another) know their inherent value, and to use their gifts in meaningful ways.

After six months of reaping the benefits of The Virtues Project both personally and professionally, I knew this was the reason I had been blessed with the Disney teacher honor. I was to share these strategies with other teachers across the United States and around the world to help them lose their own "amnesia" and empower them to help their students reach their highest potential.

But how was I going to do this? I was only one person. Of course, I did what anyone else would do -- I asked Google! I found a phone number for someone with The Virtues Project and I called her up. A local volunteer connected me to Barbara, a

Master Facilitator in California. Barbara explained that in order to have a trainer come out to do a workshop an organization had to sponsor it. However, she could tell from my enthusiasm that I was really committed and that she could trust me to find the location and people to pay her fee and expenses from California to Maryland to train us. Barbara came to Maryland in February of 2006 for the two-day "Awakening the Gifts Within" workshop, and then came back in March to offer the three-day facilitator training.

"Master Facilitator" proved to be a most accurate and well deserved title. Barbara presented the workshop powerfully, and as a result, the project really came to life for me! I knew I wanted to do this work. I planned to leave MCPS at the end of the school year and put out my shingle as a Virtues Project Facilitator, training others to utilize The Virtues Project.

A few days after Barbara returned to California she called to let me know that two of the founders of The Virtues Project, Linda Kavelin-Popov and Dr. Dan Popov, would be facilitating "A Pace of Grace" retreat for a small group of 12 people out in California. She asked me if I wanted to come and offered me the opportunity to stay at her home. Of course I wanted to come! This was a dream come true. I was so enthralled by this awesome project that the chance to be with the founders in an intimate setting was beyond my wildest dreams! So off I went to California a few weeks later.

The retreat was held in a private home in the middle of the woods in beautiful Northern California. It was a lovely, intimate setting. Once we were all seated in a circle in the living room, Dan started the first night's session with a song to honor our spirit. I have come to learn he starts every one of his talks by honoring the spirit with a song. For our first session he chose "Keep Me in Your Grace" by Kimmie Rhodes. The song starts out with the following lyrics: "Keep me in your grace, help me show the world a better face. When my voice is weak, hear my plea, sing for me. Help me to believe there's a way to be what I can't be. In life's troubled sky, be my wings, help me fly." The song touched me deep in my soul and allowed me to open up to the learning that was about to come.

For the next couple of days Linda told us many inspiring stories and facilitated a variety of multisensory experiences designed to help us learn how to Purify Our Lives, Pace Ourselves, Practice the Presence and Plan a Sustainable Life. It was exciting to hear that the Dalai Lama said, "*A Pace of Grace* contains vivid examples of how to make our daily lives meaningful. I offer my prayers that those readers who sincerely put them into practice will achieve the inner peace that is the key to lasting happiness." It has been my experience over the past several years that his statement is indeed true. I am the happiest and most peaceful I have ever been.

On the second day she took us through a guided meditation from page 226 of the book, *A Pace of Grace*. She had us visualize walking down a hallway, seeing a virtue on a door, opening the door and receiving a gift from someone. The virtue I saw was "Trust" and the gift I received was an engagement ring.

At the time I remember thinking the ring was from John Kavelin, the other founder of The Virtues Project, who was Linda's younger brother and also a Disney Imagineer. I had never met John, though we had exchanged several emails. I thought perhaps the visualization signified that we had been married in a past life or something of that nature. It was not until several years later, when I was chosen by Dan and Linda to become one of the four board members to ensure the legacy of The Virtues Project, that I really understood what that visualization was about. Remember, history chooses you? All I ever really wanted to be was an elementary school teacher and now I was Director of Education and a board member for The Virtues Project.

Throughout the entire retreat weekend I kept asking Linda questions about The Virtues Project in schools, not realizing there was a difference between *A Pace of Grace* and "The Five Strategies of The Virtues Project." Bless her patience, I was really trying it!

On the last day of the three-day retreat, Linda unveiled the latest inspirational product the founders had just finished creating. It was a set of 100 Virtues Reflection Cards to add to their collection of cards for families and schools; this new set was for personal spiritual transformation and went along with *A Pace of*

Grace. Linda asked me to be the one to pull the first card from the brand new deck and read it aloud. Excited with my hand shaking, I picked the "Purposefulness" card and, tears streaming down my cheeks, I read it. (Little did I know at the time that one of the requirements of The Virtues Project was being able to speak and cry at the same time.) I knew my purpose was The Virtues Project--this was just another confirmation.

As the retreat was wrapping up, the founders were autographing books and cards and I went up to Linda to thank her and let her know that I was committed to The Virtues Project. I was also interested in knowing if there were any job openings, and I wanted to talk with her more about some ideas I had about virtues, education and technology. I didn't realize that no one "worked" for The Virtues Project; rather, it is a movement of sorts, a global grassroots organization run by the founders and "heartcentered" virtues enthusiasts from over 100 countries around the world who volunteer as points of contact.

Linda encouraged me to learn how to balance my enthusiasm with patience, and that the best way to learn more about the project was to live The Five Strategies and apply them to my own life. Wise guidance.

After the retreat was over, Barbara and I had several hours to chat before she drove me back to the airport. I remember sitting in her car and listening to her say things like, "I honor your enthusiasm for The Virtues Project and your commitment by coming all the way out here from Maryland." When she used the virtues language, especially the word "honor" I would think to myself, *I'm on to you. I know what you are doing. You are speaking that language.*

At first I felt really uncomfortable and awkward; this was a new language—or at least a very new way of speaking. Luckily, I got used to it and was willing to grow through the discomfort to be able to receive acknowledgments as well as give them.

Fortunately the drive to the airport was two hours long. While Barbara drove I picked her brain. I wanted her to explain to me every single thing I needed to do in order to facilitate an excellent Virtues Project workshop like she had done for us just a couple of months earlier.

Even though we had a "Virtues Project Leader's Manual" which has hundreds of pages of activities, suggested materials, agendas, speaker's notes and additional resources, I much preferred Barbara walking me through, step by step, and giving me a variety of sample activities. As we said in my old technology days, "I don't like to RTFM (read the *%$#** manual!)." I wrote pages and pages of notes, capturing every creative idea she offered so generously.

I am sure she was relieved and quite exhausted by the time she finally dropped me off at the Sacramento airport. I was grateful and inspired beyond words. As I got out of the car, I thanked her for her kindness and generosity in driving me to the airport and having me spend the weekend with her. *Yes!* I thought. *I am getting the language of the virtues, and it does feel really good to acknowledge someone for the virtues they are demonstrating.* As I boarded my plane to Chicago, I reflected on all I had learned over the weekend.

Coincidence or Confirmation?

Once I landed in Chicago, I decided to sit at the first gate I came to instead of walking to the gate for Baltimore (BWI) where I would board. I knew I had about an hour to fill so I pulled out a new Wayne Dyer book called *Inspiration, Your Ultimate Calling.* The front cover has a picture of Wayne holding a blue butterfly. A butterfly is a precious symbol of mine that means transformation. In addition, I believe it is a sign from my best friend Stacey who passed away several years ago. For several months after her passing, a blue butterfly followed her mother, sister and me around. (There is much more to this story which I will save for another book.) As I opened to the first page of Wayne's book I looked up into the airport and saw David Vixie, the man who initially introduced me to The Virtues Project, walking with his wife Karen (who introduced him to the project). I could hardly contain myself.

With chills running down my spine, I quickly ran over to them, and explained that I had just come back from meeting the founders of The Virtues Project. I excitedly shared that I knew this was my calling, that I had picked the "Purposeful-ness" card from Linda's hand, and was just now sitting down to read the book *Inspiration, Your Ultimate Calling*. And then, bam, who should appear right in front of my eyes but the people who were responsible for introducing me to my calling! Oh, and by the way, David and Karen don't live in Chicago; they live in Sacramento.

Sacrifice: Giving Up Something Important for Something More Important

It was now the end of April 2006, and I had a decision to make. I knew my calling was to share The Virtues Project with other educators but it would mean a huge sacrifice. I would have to leave the classroom and school system I loved as well as 20 years worth of friendships I had made. It meant leaving a steady salary and benefits and going out on my own as a con-sultant/ businesswoman. I was sure there were many teachable moments ahead for me.

Somehow the president of our local teachers' union found out I was planning on leaving and invited me to meet her for an early breakfast one morning before school. We met at my home away from home, The Silver Diner in Rockville, MD. (They have lots of yummy organic, locally grown food and a staff that is so friendly I often go there just to get nurtured. I highly recom-mend it!)

I told the union president about my intention and the work of The Virtues Project, and she let me know that there was a half-time position for the next school year where I could do Virtues work for the school system part time and be an independent consultant the rest of the time. *Pinch me!* I thought to myself. It felt too good to be true.

I went back to school after breakfast and told my principal about my plans to leave the classroom at the end of the school year. It was bittersweet, but I was still going to be working part time in my school system. I also knew I would still be connected to my students since I had been teaching in my own neighborhood for the past five years. To this day it is such a blessing because I get to see my students as they grow up.

After the school year ended my husband and I journeyed to Canada to participate in another life changing Peak Potential event called "Wizard Training Camp." This seminar was all about the Art of Manifestation where we learned specific clearing processes to make space for higher wisdom, enlightened principles for creating success without struggle, how to tap directly into your intuition and ultimately create your deepest desires. We did things over the course of five days that, if I had not experienced myself, I never would have believed they were possible.

On the last day we had to set another intention. No longer a skeptic, I enthusiastically set my intention: To get The Virtues Project into all public schools across the US by 2012. I had to believe it with 100% of my being. My husband set an intention of creating Livability Centers all over the country. He had to believe it with 100% of his mind, heart and soul. Because we both believed with 100% of our being that each was possible, we were able to physically do something, which under normal circumstances would have been nearly impossible. (I wish I could give you the specifics, however I made the commitment not to share this with anyone in case you participate in the program; it might prevent you from having a similar life changing experience.)

Once again we left the seminar totally inspired! On the airplane back from Canada my husband and I started working on my business plan. We laid out a great deal of information. When I got home I created my own Limited Liability Company (LLC), The Heart of Education.

The new school year started and I began my new job. Although I was supposed to be doing Virtues Project facilitation, I found myself working with teachers who were working towards their National Board Certification. I had achieved my certification a few years prior and knew the steadfast commitment this endeavor took. At any other time in my career I would have loved to work and support these committed, excellent educators, but that was not my calling now. I needed to get clarity about my job description, and was finally able to set up a meeting for Monday, October 9, 2006, with the president of the teachers' union to find out if we had had a misunderstanding.

On Thursday, October 5, 2006, I was working out at the gym (before going to the Diner and then heading off to work). While on the elliptical with Kenny Loggins blasting in my ears, I noticed from the corner of my eye on the TV monitor that there was going to be a school safety summit with President Bush and Education Secretary Spellings. I immediately called a friend of mine who is a reporter for "Ed Week," and asked her if she knew anything about the summit.

She did a little investigating and then called me back to let me know the summit was "invitation only" and was being held at the 4 H Center in Chevy Chase, Maryland the following Tuesday. So I called the founders of The Virtues Project and explained the opportunity I saw. I asked them, if I could get us an invitation to attend this summit, would one of them come from Western Canada to Maryland to go with me? Since John was heading to New York that Monday anyway, he agreed to come directly to Maryland instead.

Now how to get an invite to meet the President of the United States and the Secretary of Education? I called my dad, my biggest supporter in the world, and asked him if he would ask his best friend, who was an ambassador to one of the European countries at the time, if he could get a letter to the White House ASAP requesting an invite. Of course he said yes, so Linda and I crafted a letter and sent it to the White House on Friday, October 6, 2006, and prayed it would get to the powers that be in time.

Monday morning I went to the gym and then to the Diner as usual. As I was leaving I bumped into one of the associate school superintendents, whom I love and respect dearly, and asked him how he was. He said fine, though it looked as if NCLB had drained his passion for education right out of him. My heart sank and I felt so sad for him.

He then asked me how I was and I believe I shocked us both when I said, "I think I am going to resign today." I know the words came out of my mouth, but I did not know how they got there! As I drove home to shower before heading off to work I was crying but also companioning myself by asking *What's happening? What are those tears for? What virtue will help you? What's clearer to you now?*

What was happening is that I knew I had to take the full leap of faith. The tears were for the sadness of leaving a school system I loved. The virtues I needed were Faith, Trust and Courage. What was clear was that I needed to resign. Oh boy, this was going to be an interesting day.

So off to work I headed. We were having a meeting that day to discuss how our school system was doing in our efforts to earn the Malcolm Baldrige Award. The Baldrige Award "promotes awareness of performance excellence as an increasingly important element in competitiveness. It also promotes the sharing of successful performance strategies and the benefits derived from using these strategies. To receive a Baldrige Award, an organization must have a role-model organizational management system that ensures continuous improvement in delivering products and/ or services, demonstrates efficient and effective operations, and provides a way of engaging and responding to customers and other stakeholders."

We were discussing how our actions were aligned throughout the school system and, although we were committed to excellence, I could not help but to think about the huge area I felt we were not addressing. I was one of 140 instructional specialists and not one was assigned to character education or social emotional learning. I felt that as a school system this was one of the most important areas we should be focused on.

I was so frustrated! Most of the time I felt as if I was the only one who knew or at least cared that many of today's graduates do not have the 21st Century Skills necessary to be successful in the work place, let alone in life. We have missed the mark in education of nurturing the *Emotional Intelligences* (Goleman 2005) of our young people. We have been narrowly focused on academic rigor, which only translates into 20% of what students need to know and be able to do as successful employees. According to Daniel Goleman, it is our EQ, the effective awareness, control and management of one's own emotions, and those of other people, that makes up 80% of what we need in order to be successful, not our IQ.

When we had our morning break I went outside to check my voicemail and sure enough I had received our invitation to the following day's meeting with President Bush and Secretary Spellings. After break, when I returned to the table where my cohort met monthly, I told them I thought they might not see me at future meetings. I was right.

The meeting ended and I left to pick up John Kavelin from Union Station in DC. On the way downtown, I stopped by the union office to talk to the president of the teachers' union to see if we had a misunderstanding about my job. She said we did, so I simply said, "I resign." Looking back I wish I had been more patient and had taken the time to talk through it. However, the reality was likely that the only way I would have been able to make a break from the school system at that time was to do it without thinking. Though I am sorry for any harm I may have caused and for the extra work I left for the partners on my team, and for possibly letting some wonderful folks down, I did what I felt I had to in order to remain true to myself and my passion. I am committed to making living amends by being of service to the school system in any way I can.

Purposefulness

Purposefulness is being aware that each of us is here for a reason. We value our lives by discovering the part we are uniquely meant to play. We discern our intention and focus on it mindfully. We visualize it happening. We set goals and achieve them step by step, resisting distractions. We give each task single-minded concentration and excellence. We invest our full enthusiasm into even the simplest job. In the flow of our lives, there are many turns and unexpected events. Within it all, there are lessons to be learned and gifts to receive. Purposefulness is trusting the journey.

The Virtues Project™

1 What is your life's purpose?
2 What is your big dream, how do you wish to make your mark on the world?
3 What do you need to learn and/or be willing to sacrifice to be able to live it?

Chapter Three

The Road Taken

"Two roads diverged in a wood, and I,
I took the one less traveled by,
And that has made all the difference."
Robert Frost

So now I was without a job and on my way to pick up one of the founders of The Virtues Project. At this time, my latest intention was to become an integral part of The Virtues Project, though I still did not really understand that no one "worked" for the Project. After driving by the Washington Monument, the White House, and the US Capitol, I pulled up to Union Station and John got into my car.

After a warm embrace and thanking him for his flexibility and willingness to come to DC instead of going to NY, we began our drive up Massachusetts Avenue to my home in Maryland. About ten minutes into the drive I finally said, "I resigned today." He said, "Good, now that means you can be Director of Education for The Virtues Project." I said, "Great!" He said, "But we don't have any money to pay you." I said, "Still Great! I was going to do the work of The Virtues Project any way, and now I have the direct support of the founders."

In the back of my mind I was thinking about a conversation I had several months earlier with my younger brother Devin, a gifted entrepreneur, loving father, and extremely generous person. He told me that he was about to come into some money and offered to give me some. He wanted to know how much I needed and what I would use it for. At the time I did not know but said I would get back to him. I contacted my brother and asked if John and I could meet with him after we met with the President and Secretary of Education and of course he said, "Yes."

John and I were on fire after the School Safety Summit as we headed over to my brother's office. I had addressed Madame Secretary, and John had a lively discussion with the President. We met so many like-minded individuals, such as Craig Scott from Rachel's Challenge, who immediately saw the value of The Virtues Project and agreed that the key to school safety was about changing the culture, not adding more armed guards and metal detectors.

When we arrived at Devin's office, he greeted us warmly and invited us to sit down. As different as Devin and I are, we have many important similarities. One of the more interesting ones is that we are both fans of Coach Wooden. Devin's office reflected his own successes: a framed picture of Coach's Success Pyramid, precious photos of his beautiful family, a photo of him as an escort during the 1984 Olympics and one of him finishing the New York Marathon.

My brother has had experiences that many people have never even dreamed of, and through his generosity, has afforded those less fortunate with opportunities beyond their wildest dreams including money to start up non-profits and scholarships to attend the University of Pennsylvania. Surely my brother was going to display his generosity once again.

I introduced John and Devin, and then I told my brother that I had resigned from MCPS. Next, I shared with him that I knew what I wanted the money for and how much I needed. I was hoping he would pay my salary for a year so I could get the Director of Education for The Virtues Project position up and running. My heart sank as I heard the deafening word "No" pass from my brother's lips. I was confused, horrified and embarrassed. Here I was with one of the founders of The Virtues Project, a project honored by The United Nations and endorsed by the Dalai Lama, helping to bring out the best in ourselves and others, in over 100 countries and my own brother said, "No."

This was inconceivable to me. When I finally mustered the courage to ask why, Devin said he didn't see how The Virtues Project could make any money. His bottom line was about making money. I was at such a loss for words that I had no response. I wish I would have had the where-with-all to say, "The Virtues Project's bottom line is about making a difference to humanity." Dazed and confused, we left Devin's office without his financial support, but my passion and commitment to this work were even stronger.

I have come to understand that my brother's refusal to support my request for money at that time was wise discernment on his part. He really had my best interest at heart, though I was too emotional to realize it then. My brother plays the role of one of my spiritual personal trainers, engaging in a variety of interactions and experiences where I get to learn about and strengthen my feelings of worthiness.

Things Happen for a Reason

I can honestly say I am truly grateful that my brother said no to my request seven years ago because it forced me to grow. I am forever grateful for his generosity of support, time and money over the past several years. He and my husband, bless their patience with me, have been coaching me through the process of becoming an entrepreneur.

Devin has given me many amazing resources to read, introductions to awesome people, funded the development of my www.giftsofcharacter.org site, taken me to the YPO (Young Presidents Organization) Global Summit, led Dave and me through a wonderful retreat (or as he calls it an advancement), been incredibly generous with his money and much more.

For the first several years after I left MCPS, I found it very difficult to identify with being an entrepreneur because I thought I had to give up my identity as a teacher to become a businesswoman. One of Devin's favorite quotes by Jim Collins is "To give up the Tyranny of the OR to embrace the Genius of the AND." Just recently I have come to embrace the "Genius of the AND" and have invested much time, money and energy in developing the skills and strategies to strengthen the scalability and sustainability of The Virtues Project through my work with Bradley Communication's Quantum Leap Program.

Devin's initial answer of no actually caused me to "learn how to fish." I am still learning and sometimes it can be really lonely, hard and hot waiting for something to bite; however, I trust the process will be well worth it. In fact it already has been in many ways. For one, I would never have written this book!

Devin's Call and My Calling

Over the past couple of years there has been a positive shift in my relationship with my brother. He has become more spiritual and I have become more business-minded. As a result, I feel we have a greater understanding and mutual respect for one another.

Two summers ago Devin called me on my cell and said, "Hey Sis, you have to read Ted's new book (Ted Leonsis, former Vice Chairman of AOL, owner of the Washington Capitals and the Washington Wizards, filmmaker and philanthropist). It's called *The Business of Happiness: 6 Secrets to Extraordinary Success in Work and Life*. He explained, "The first three common practices he talks about are all about me and the last three, gratitude, empathy and higher calling, are all about you." Then he read the line from Ted's introduction that said, "The happiest among us are the people who find that mission, whether it is finding a cure for cancer or... teaching children the practice of virtue."

Needless to say I bought the book and began reading it that day. I was so inspired by Ted's commitment to making the world a better place and the generosity and sincerity with which he lives, works and plays, that I felt compelled to stop reading in the middle of page 195 to connect and send him an email. I wanted to let him know how grateful I was and to say that I am one of those happy people because I have the honor of teaching not just children the practice of virtue, but adults as well.

Ted and I exchanged a few emails and I even had the opportunity to pitch my Caps for Character Campaign to his VP of Marketing.

The purpose of my Caps for Character Campaign was to:

- Increase engagement with fans on and off the ice
- Increase positive impact of the Caps as an organization
- Increase positive press for Caps, great opportunity to learn and show their values in practice
- Increase player's performance

The idea was basically that fans would follow players on and off the ice throughout each season looking for the qualities of character they exemplify. Towards the end of the season fans would vote online for the player that most exemplifies integrity, excellence, unity, cooperation, etc. A special package of TOPPS trading cards would be created highlighting the virtue, a brief definition and how the player exemplified the virtue. This could also be done league-wide where the Caps take responsibility for initiating this. It could be done with youth leagues and high schools as well. Unfortunately, my idea never took hold with the Caps, but I trust that there is a sports organization out there that this will resonate with and make it a reality.

Over the past few years my business strategy has been similar to my cooking. I would make spaghetti, throw a piece of it onto the ceiling and see if it stuck. If it did, then it was ready. Similarly, I would generously toss myself and The Virtues Project materials around and would pray that something would stick so that I could sustain myself doing the work I cherish.

I have had the good fortune of having many wonderful experiences doing workshops, retreats and keynotes around the world and learning to refine my business skills in order to be of greater service to The Virtues Project worldwide community and to humanity as a whole. I created an online introduction for the National Education Association (NEA), created an iPhone app for the Virtues Reflection Cards and Educator Cards (which are more legible on an iPad because of its size) put on a global mentorship with facilitators from all over the world and am working with an over-the-top diligent webmaster to create The Virtues Project Affiliate Program.

Holding out Hope

We have incredible testimonials from around the world about how the five simple strategies of The Virtues Project bring out the best in both students and educators. Attendance increases because students feel safe, valued and connected. Student achievement increases because students embrace 21st Century Skills, have higher authentic self-esteem and are more confident in learning. Discipline referrals decrease because students feel heard and do not need to act out for attention. Bullies are often transformed into leaders. The overall climate of the school is more peaceful and joyful, resulting in less stress for everyone and allowing staff and students to thrive.

As great as these testimonials are, as an educator I have always known that we needed to do some serious research. When I first got involved with The Virtues Project, I had the honor of working with Barbara Mackenzie, a passionate and creative facilitator from Canada on The Virtues Project Research Task Force. A few years later, I had the privilege of working with Dorrie Hancock, a brilliant scholar who moved from Papua New Guinea to around the corner from me and who became one of my closest friends and mentors. For years we looked for research grants that aligned with our work, and a school system that would partner with us. The John Templeton Foundation seemed to be the perfect organization; however, you have to be invited to submit. Dorrie was diligently working on her PhD when her husband, who worked for the World Bank, was transferred again and off they went to Mongolia. I was back at square one with the research and no idea what to do next.

Grace Steps In

After working and pushing hard to get some research going with The Virtues Project, I finally surrendered and decided to facilitate

"A Pace of Grace: Virtues for a Sustainable Life" retreat instead. "A Pace of Grace" is a four-part program that offers lessons to re-discover the essential elements of a life well lived. It is really help-ful for those of us who are "e-type personalities," we do every-thing for everyone else without taking care of ourselves. I worked with Martie, another Virtues Project facilitator, and we held the retreat at the Am Kolel Sanctuary out in the country, about 45 minutes north of Washington DC. During the planning phase of the retreat, the sanctuary director became interested in attending and invited one of her friends, Laura, to attend as well.

We had a wonderful group that weekend, with people from all different backgrounds and professions attending.

When the retreat concluded on Sunday afternoon, there were three participants who refused to go home until I made the commitment to schedule a two-day introduction to The Vir-tues Project as well as a three-day Facilitator Training. Tammy and Nancy were two of those people. They ended up being the educators who were featured in the NEA course. Laura was the third person and she invited me to "ChildTrends" to give an overview of The Virtues Project to her team of researchers during lunch. That was all ChildTrends needed to get on board to become research champions for The Virtues Project.

After several failed attempts to attain a research grant with the United States Department of Education (USDE), we were finally invited to submit a grant to the John Templeton Founda-tion. There was a large team of researchers from "ChildTrends" and everyone worked tirelessly to create a sound proposal. I thought we had this in the bag. It was Templeton after all, and they were all about virtues! I will never forget opening the email the day after Christmas 2011 which said our proposal had been rejected. I cried for four hours straight, wailing from the depths of my soul, and feeling like a Who down In Whoville. *Why wasn't anyone listening! Didn't they know how important this research was to the future of education and to the future of humanity!* Once I finally emerged from my crying spell, I remembered that things happen for a reason and I realized that this rejection just meant that something better was going to come. I was sure of it, but what was it?

A Dream Come True: A Return to the Castle

A couple months later I was at a Bullying Symposium put on by MCPS, my old school district. There were a variety of stakeholders from around the community, and a panel of experts on bullying. Toward the end of the symposium a young woman came running up to me and said that we needed to talk because her school really needed The Virtues Project. I had met this woman several years earlier when I was in the "spaghetti" phase of business development. Her name was Tamar and I had met with her when she was an assistant principal at a different school. I had given her a variety of Virtues materials including the Educator Cards, Reflection Cards and *Educator's Guide*. We exchanged contact information and later that evening I got an email from her requesting that we get together.

The following Saturday we met at her office and she shared with me the history of what was happening at her school and the vision that the staff had for creating a part-time position focused on character education. She said she was interested in having me return to Greencastle Elementary School--the Castle--to help create a more positive culture with The Virtues Project. I had taught third grade there 19 years earlier when I was pregnant with my son Jake. Needless to say I was ecstatic--how perfect! I would be doing character development part-time back in MCPS, in one school, working one day a week as a consultant for the Character Education Partnership which has a national focus, and the rest of the time doing The Virtues Project on a global scale. My arrows were all facing towards the same direction and my different roles informed the practice of one another. What a gift.

I really missed being part of a school system and now that MCPS had a new superintendent whose vision I believed in, it was "safe" to come home. Dr. Starr, the new superintendent, has been known to say that he would rather "we create great kids and just good students, than great students and just OK kids."

After going through the interview process, filling out all of the forms as well as taking a 13-step salary decrease since I had given up my tenure six years earlier when I resigned, I was finally back as an MCPS employee and the character development coach at Greencastle ES. I was psyched.

On my first official day back in MCPS, we had an offsite training. As I was following the directions on my GPS and singing inspiring songs at the top of my lungs with tears of gratitude streaming down my face that I was home at last, I started getting a funny feeling. No way, this would be too coincidental, impossible, it couldn't be! As I approached the intersection, put on my blinker, made a left turn into the parking lot and looked at the building numbers in front of me, I could hardly believe it. I was sitting in front of the exact same building I had been in the day I resigned six years before! Chills went up my spine. I parked the car, got out, connected with my team and went inside the building. Once inside I was met with several curious looks from familiar people who were no doubt wondering what I was doing there. Many were surprised when I told them I was back in MCPS for the fourth time.

After catching up for a few minutes we went into the auditorium. My team and I went down to sit in the front. Dr. Starr opened his talk by asking, "How many of you think we test too much?" Everyone's hands went up. Then he said the words I will never forget, "I am all about social and emotional learning and character development." I burst into tears for the second time that day. *Could it be true? Had I come full circle?* The reason I left six years earlier was because I was on a team of 140 instructional specialists and none were assigned to social and emotional learning and character development. Now here was the new Superintendent stating that that was his focus. Finally I was back in the county, doing The Virtues Project in my old school, under the leadership of amazing administrators, working with a warm and committed staff and parent community. This was a dream come true!

Zeal

Zeal is passion for a purpose we deeply value. We follow a vision of what is possible with enthusiasm and ardor. When we are zealous, we give our all. Zeal is fueled by our belief and faith. We do all that we can to serve a cause we believe to be real and true. We need tolerance as the ballast for our zeal when others' beliefs differ from our own. Zeal is being for something, not against anything. Zeal is the fire in our belly. It illumines even the smallest task with joy.

The Virtues Project™

1 Do you believe things happen for a reason?
2 What experiences have you had that you KNOW are not co-incidences?
3 What are you most passionate about?

Chapter Four

Gifts of Character

"Intelligence plus character - that is the goal of true education."
Martin Luther King, Jr.

True Education Reform and The Whole Child

We hear a lot these days about education reform, but what does it really mean?

The pressures on our schools, educators and students are at an all-time high. School violence and bullying continue to escalate. The dropout rate is staggering at more than 30%. The tensions of increased academic rigor add pressure to an already challenged system. School populations are becoming increasingly diverse, and as schools suffer from dwindling fiscal resources, they are expected to do more for less. Federal testing mandates often overwhelm both teachers and students. Such tensions threaten the security, safety, progress and peace of our schools.

There are many education reformers out there who believe the way to help students achieve increasingly high expectations is to push them harder and faster, and do even more testing. I absolutely agree that having high expectations is essential. However, I don't believe that we get to that truth about what kids need to know and be able to do through more and more testing. For me, I feel that the Association for Supervision and Curriculum Development (ASCD) really has it right with the Whole Child Compact. Their "Learning Compact Redefined: A

Call to Action" was a response to No Child Left Behind. Commission co-chairs Stephanie Pace Marshall and Hugh B. Price write, "This report provides the impetus for educators and policymakers, parents, community leaders and other stakeholders to change the conversation about learning and schooling from reforming its structures to transforming its condition so that each child can develop his strengths and restore his unique capacities for intellectual, social, emotional, physical and spiritual learning.

"When we commit to educating all children within the context of whole communities and whole schools, we commit to designing learning environments that weave together the threads that connect not only math, science, the arts and humanities but also mind, heart, body and spirit - connection that tend to be fragmented in our current approach."

If you talk to educators who are actually on the front lines-- in classrooms working with students, the administrators of schools--what you will find is that we are all basically saying the same thing. In Clifton Taulbert's book *Eight Habits of the Heart for Educators*, he talks about children being "the future trustees of our communities, and that how we view them and what we expect will make all the difference in how they view themselves and how they welcome and meet awesome tasks ahead of them. It will make all the difference in the future of our nation."

Clifton goes on to say, "What's missing from our schools today is a positive vision of our students to drive our efforts and the courage to build the kind of community that will make the most of their potential." He left Tupelo, Mississippi, determined to use his voice to make sure that "we do not through conversations, perspective, and loads of social data, negatively brand our children." That is exactly what he's gone on to do as a leader in the character education movement.

What is Character Education Anyway?

According to The Character Education Partnership (CEP), "Character education is a national movement encouraging schools to create environments that foster ethical, responsible, and caring young people. It is the intentional, proactive effort by schools, districts, and states to instill in their students important core, ethical values that we all share such as caring, honesty, fairness, responsibility, and respect for self and others.

"Effective character education is comprehensive; it is integrated into all aspects of classroom life, including academic subjects and infused throughout the school day in all areas of the school (playing field, cafeteria, hallways, school buses, etc.). It provides long-term solutions that address moral, ethical, and academic issues that are of growing concern about our society and the safety of our schools."

As a result of No Child Left Behind, schools have become so focused on academic rigor and meeting Annual Yearly Progress (AYP) that we have forgotten what the true purpose of education is all about... to create whole, thoughtful, creative, collaborative, compassionate and caring individuals, who are independent and critical thinkers that positively contribute to humanity.

Character Education Can Make the Difference

In this climate of stress, schools need tremendous support to focus on the traditional goals that are their true purpose, namely helping students become smart and helping them become good. Society needs a competent, skilled workforce and citizens who also care for the common good. "The Smart and Good High Schools Report" (Lickona & Davidson, 2005) points out that performance character requires the development of virtues such as "a strong work ethic, a positive attitude, and perseverance," and that moral character requires the development of virtues such as "integrity, respect, cooperation, and justice." The report also advocates that these qualities of character be systemic throughout the school and, indeed, whole school districts.

Last century thinking asserted that performance character was the domain of schools and moral character the domain of families, but this impaired the ability of both school and home to provide excellent education to our children.

On this issue the United States Department of Education (2001) wrote, "Character education... is our shared responsibility... Character education is a learning process that enables students and adults in a school community to understand, care about and act on core ethical values such as respect, justice, civic virtue, citizenship, and responsibility for self and others. Upon such core values, we form the attitudes and actions that are the hallmark of safe, healthy and informed communities that serve as the foundation of our society."

The good news as we enter this new millennium is the nation is aspiring to a more holistic view that goes beyond a narrowed focus on academic considerations.

The 11 Principles of Effective Character Education

The Character Education Partnership created 11 Principles as a foundational framework for what works in character education. According to CEP, "There is no single script for effective character education, but there are some important basic principles. The following 11 Principles serve as guidelines that schools and other groups can use to plan a character education effort. They can be used in conjunction with CEP's Character Education Quality Standards to evaluate available character education programs, books, and curriculum resources."

Principle 1:   Promotes core ethical values as the basis of good character.

Principle 2:   Defines "character" comprehensively to include thinking, feeling, and behavior.

Principle 3:   Uses a comprehensive, intentional, proactive, and effective approach to character development.

Principle 4:   Creates a caring school community.

Principle 5:   Provides students with opportunities for moral action.

Principle 6:   Includes a meaningful and challenging academic curriculum that respects all learners, develops their character, and helps them to succeed.

Principle 7:   Strives to foster students' self-motivation.

Principle 8:   Engages the school staff as a learning and moral community that shares responsibility for charac-

ter education and attempts to adhere to the same
core values that guide the education of students.

Principle 9: Fosters shared moral leadership and long-range support of the character education initiative.

Principle 10: Engages families and community members as partners in the character-building effort.

Principle 11: Evaluates the character of the school, the school staff's functioning as character educators, and the extent to which students manifest good character.

Positive Effects of Character Education

Research by CEP found the following list of positive effects of quality character education.

- Improved school culture and climate
- Improved academic performance
- Improved behavior by students
- Improved moral reasoning
- Improved sense of belonging
- Reduced violence in schools
- Improved identification with school
- Reduced substance abuse
- Improved problem solving skills
- Improved emotional competency
- Reduced acts of risky behaviors
- Increased helping behavior by students

Who wouldn't want these outcomes in their school?

Social and Emotional Learning and 21st Century Skills

Business leaders across the US say that many of today's graduates do not have the 21st Century Skills necessary to be successful in the workplace, let alone in life.

According to an article in *Business Week*, "Companies are finding new ways to differentiate themselves and create entirely new markets... many are finding that in an intensely networked age, cooperation works better than direct competition" (Solomon & Schrum 2007). So what does that mean for our schools? Instead of encouraging competition for the highest GPAs, APs and SATs, we need to support our students in developing both their performance character and their moral character. We do not need to create any more business folks with the ethics of Enron, nor do we need to create teachers and doctors who are kind and compassionate people but unable to demonstrate excellence within their profession.

In the book entitled *Promoting Social and Emotional Learning: Guidelines for Educators*, the authors describe social emotional competence as "the ability to understand, manage, and express the social and emotional aspects of one's life in ways that enable the successful management of life tasks such as learning, forming relationships, solving everyday problems, and adapting to the complex demands of growth and development. Self-awareness, control of impulsivity, working cooperatively, and caring about oneself and others' social emotional learning is the process through which children and adults develop the skills and attitudes and values necessary to acquire social and emotional competence."

So what's the difference between character education and social and emotional learning? Maurice Elias, editor of *Promoting Social and Emotional Learning: Guidelines for Educators* and a professor at Rutgers University, explains social-emotional and character development (SECD) as simply a more recent version of social and emotional learning (SEL).

Tom Lickona, often referred to as the grandfather of character education and author of *Character Matters*, responds to the question often asked by educators, "If we invest time and energy in developing a character education program, will student learning improve?" Tom's answer to that question is a confident "yes" as long as two conditions are met. First, he says, academic learning will improve if the school's character education program improves the quality of human relationships between adults and kids and kids and each other, thereby improving the environment for teaching and learning. Second, he says that character education efforts need to include a strong academic program that teaches students the skills and habits of working hard and making the most of their education.

Positive Psychology

So where is positive psychology in all of this? Dr. Martin Seligman, author of *Authentic Happiness*, describes how traditional psychology focuses on problems and how to "fix" them, whereas positive psychology focuses on strengths. He goes on to make the comparison between strengths and virtues, explaining that the criteria for strengths are: "They are valued in almost every culture. They are valued in their own right, not just as a means to other ends. They are malleable." He goes on to say "that even though psychology has neglected virtue, religion and philosophy have not."

In his book *Learned Optimism: How to Change Your Mind and Your Life*, Dr. Seligman describes three different forms of happiness that you can pursue. "For the Pleasant Life, you aim to have as much positive emotion as possible and learn the skills to amplify positive emotion. For the Engaged Life, you identify your highest strengths and talents and recraft your life to use them as much as you can in work, love, friendship, parenting and leisure. For the Meaningful Life, you use your highest strengths and talents to belong to and serve something you believe is larger than the self."

Virtues and Values

When I first began facilitating Virtues Project workshops for educators in 2006, participants would hear the word "virtue" and many would immediately put up a wall. What comes to mind when you hear the word virtue? Do you associate it with a specific religion or political party? Do you think that there's some kind of judgment associated with it? Those are some of responses I have gotten in the past. Now, in 2012 I am finding that educators are thirsty for the virtues and very open to using them in the classroom.

The Virtues Project's definition of the word "virtues" is as follows: "Virtues are universal positive qualities of character." Virtues are the very meaning and purpose of our lives, the content of our character and the truest expression of our souls. For people of all cultures, ethnicities and beliefs, they are the essence of authentic success. Virtue means power, strength, inner quality. Virtues are the content of our character, the elements of the human spirit. They grow stronger whenever we use them. As a six-yearold once said, "Virtues are what's good about us."

Values, on the other hand, can be culture or group specific and aren't necessarily character qualities. Think about some of the things that are important to you. Do you value time and money? How about family? All virtues can be values, but not all values can necessarily be virtues.

Take a look at the list of words below. Keep in mind that virtues are "universal positive qualities of character." Are there any words on this list that you think don't fall into that category? (Come on, be honest!)

Assertiveness	Forgiveness	Orderliness
Caring	Friendliness	Patience
Cleanliness	Generosity	Peacefulness
Commitment	Gentleness	Perseverance
Compassion	Helpfulness	Purposefulness
Confdence	Honesty	Reliability
Consideration	Honor	Respect
Cooperation	Humility	Responsibility
Courage	Idealism	Self-discipline
Courtesy	Integrity	Service
Creativity	Joyfulness	Tact Thankfulness
Detachment	Justice	Tolerance
Determination	Kindness	Trust
Diligence	Love	Trustworthiness
Enthusiasm	Loyalty	Truthfulness
Excellence	Moderation	Understanding
Flexibility	Modesty	Unity

How about "detachment"? Oftentimes people will see the word detachment and think that it means not caring, or separate or apart from something or someone. Not sure how it would that be a virtue? Read the virtue card of detachment at the end of this chapter and see if it resonates with you.

Perhaps now can you see how detachment is a virtue, maybe even one you would like to possess more of. You might even like the people that you work with, live with and encounter on a regular basis to possess this virtue. If you think about it, you can see that it's really an essential life skill. If we could just call on detachment more often, not take things so personally, think how much more peaceful the world would be, and how much more serenity would fill our lives. I encourage you to read the virtue of detachment every day and be reminded that you have the choice to use thinking and feeling together every day to inform the choices you make.

Potential

We are all born with all of the virtues in us in potential. It is our life experiences, as well as our relationships, that help us develop our virtues. We have strength virtues, those virtues that are easy for us to call on. We also have growth virtues, the virtues that don't come naturally to us. My strength virtue is "enthusiasm." When I was shopping for my virtues I may have gone down the enthusiasm aisle a few too many times! My enthusiasm gives me energy to do the work that I believe in, however sometimes I can be so enthusiastic that I can drive people crazy. However, I've been learning to balance my enthusiasm with my growth virtue of patience. It's essential for us to be mindful of how our strength virtue shows up in our behaviors, and when it's important to work on developing our growth virtues. But the good news is we don't have to do this work alone.

If we develop the potential of the virtues within us, how can we strengthen them? One way is to do a "virtues pick" every day. Each day randomly select a virtue, read about it and then try to see how you use or don't use that virtue throughout the day. You will be surprised how much you learn about yourself, not to mention others, when you focus on just one virtue. I invite you to visit www. virtuesproject.org where you can choose from a variety of sets of electronic virtues cards. On my homepage are personal Reflection Cards that adults and high school students can use to strengthen their virtues. On my Education page you can find cards that are developmentally appropriate for younger students. There are other cards on my Family page to use at home with your own children.

In an article by Chris Chrisman in the *Peninsula Gazette* from the University of Pennsylvania, he writes about a young assistant professor of psychology, Angela Duckworth, a 2006 graduate. She talks about how reformers and policy makers point to sub-par teachers and inadequate principals as well as single parenthood and other demographic drags including health, nutrition and intangible handicaps of poverty as being those things that really impact student achievement.

However, she believes that failure of students to acquire basic skills was not attributable to the difficulty of the material or to the students' lack of intelligence or any of the factors mentioned above. Her intuition told her that the real problem was character. Paul Tough also writes about Angela's work in his book and her research on grit.

So the big issue is how do we develop character, in ourselves, and in our students? This is the crux of this book. The Five Strategies of The Virtues Project are an excellent approach to how we can best develop, strengthen and appreciate the character qualities in ourselves and others.

The first thing to consider is how virtues play out in our everyday lives. By focusing conscious awareness on recognizing the virtues in everyday life, it is easy to see how they affect our actions in everything that we do.

Let's take a look at a very real and relevant concern: bullying. If we look at some of the character qualities of a bully, what might we find? Oftentimes they have incredible leadership skills, but use their power and ability to control for violence. If we were to invite them to use power with compassion and responsibility, then instead of being a bully, they become leaders. I have witnessed many bullies transformed into leaders in the schools where I have worked. Helping students become aware of their power and teaching them that incorporating compassion and responsibility is a choice is often all they need to turn themselves around.

One of the ways to start thinking about and appreciating virtues in your own life is to do a virtues interview. The virtues interview that follows was taken from *The Virtues Project Educators' Guide* on page 43. If you have a friend or colleague that you can share this with I encourage you to do so. If not, you can do it as a personal reflection for yourself.

Virtues Interview

Directions: Choose a partner and take turns interviewing one another. Do not write or take notes. Just be present and listen.

1   Name someone you admire. This person may be a figure in history or a person in your life. What is the core virtue this person practices? What attracts you to this virtue?

2   Name one of your own strength virtues, one that is strong and well-developed in you. Say a few words about how you live it.

3   Name a virtue you would like to grow, one that is underdeveloped in you. Say a few words about how it is needed in your life.

4   What is one of the biggest challenges in your life right now? What virtue would help you meet that challenge?

5   What are your hopes for the semester?

6   What is a source of joy in your life at this time?

7   Virtues Acknowledgment: Interviewer, please give your partner a virtues acknowledgment by telling him/her a virtue you notice in him/her and specifically how you see it.

" I want to acknowledge you for the virtue of _____ and the way you show it is _____."

This interactive interview activity is wonderful to use with students at the beginning of the school year to help them learn about one another and themselves. *The Educator's Guide* has several other meaningful and creative activities for helping students deepen their understanding of the virtues and themselves.

World-renowned Stanford University psychologist Carol Dweck talks about the difference between a "growth" mindset and a "fix" mindset set in her book *Mindset – The New Psychology of Success*. Dr. Dweck says that "Mindsets are beliefs—beliefs about yourself and your most basic qualities. Think about your intelligence, your talents, your personality. Are these qualities simply fixed traits or are they things you can cultivate throughout your life?

"The growth mindset, the understanding of intelligence and abilities as qualities we can develop, has been shown over and over to have powerful ramifications on student motivation and learning, and school success. When teachers and students focus on improvement rather than on whether they're smart, kids learn a lot more." When we use the language of virtues by acknowledging the virtue and providing the evidence we see in students, it helps them to strengthen their growth mindset.

In addition when we offer guidance and correction and talk in terms of an invitation back to a virtue, that also helps to strengthen a students' growth mindset. We learn not to say, "Wow I see you are stuck with that problem, maybe you just need to work harder." Instead we invite them to a virtue such as, "Wow, I see your determination in the way that you are working on that hard problem without giving up." That lets them know that they have the determination in them and that it is a choice to call on. It becomes a transferable skill they can use when things in life are hard.

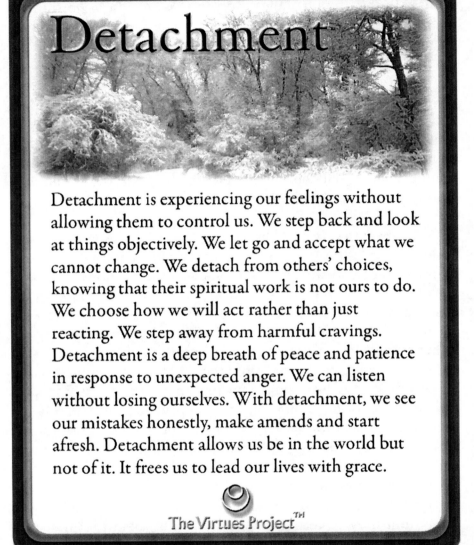

Detachment

Detachment is experiencing our feelings without allowing them to control us. We step back and look at things objectively. We let go and accept what we cannot change. We detach from others' choices, knowing that their spiritual work is not ours to do. We choose how we will act rather than just reacting. We step away from harmful cravings. Detachment is a deep breath of peace and patience in response to unexpected anger. We can listen without losing ourselves. With detachment, we see our mistakes honestly, make amends and start afresh. Detachment allows us be in the world but not of it. It frees us to lead our lives with grace.

The Virtues Project™

1 What does true education reform mean to you?
2 What relevance do you feel character education and social emotional learning have in education today?
3 If you had the opportunity to create the ideal teaching and learning community that supports the Whole Child, what would it look like, sound like and feel like?

Chapter Five

Change Your Language: Change Your Life

See Me Beautiful
by Red and Kathy Grammer

See me beautiful
Look for the best in me
It's what I really am
And all I want to be
It may take some time
It may be hard to find
But see me beautiful

See me beautiful
Each and every day
Could you take a chance
Could you find a way
To see me shining through
In everything I do
And see me beautiful

The Committee

We have all heard the old adage "whether you think you can or you can't, you're right." I think this applies to Carol Dweck's work as well. I have also had some personal experiences with the power of the language that I feel are important to share. After I had been using the language and strategies of the virtues for a while, I was down in Miami with my brother at a Young Presidents' Organization (YPO) Global Conference. I had been in sessions all day when I felt the need to get out of the hotel and go for a walk.

So there I was, walking on the boardwalk in Miami Beach when I noticed lots of cat food scattered around. I thought to myself, *Why is all of this cat food on the boardwalk?* Then I realized there were lots of homeless cats, and I thought, *Ohhhhhh, look at all this cat food, it must be compassion that these people have for these cats.* Soon after I looked up and saw somebody pushing someone in a wheel chair and I thought to myself... *service.* As I walked I continued to notice all that was around me. I saw a couple walking down the boardwalk holding hands and I thought to myself... *love.* Then I saw somebody pick something up and hand it to someone else... *helpfulness.* I looked out into the ocean and I felt awe; I couldn't get the virtues out of my mind. I realized once I had committed to using this language, not only did it change how I acted in the world, it also changed how I viewed the world.

Instead of "taking people's inventories" and judging them on what they do not have or what they are doing negatively, I was now seeing them in light of their virtues. Now I often get to look underneath the behavior at the virtue that they are really demonstrating. If I am in a meeting and somebody gets really angry I know they are really passionate or committed to whatever it is they are trying to share with us.

A few years ago, the founders of The Virtues Project asked me to be on a TV show for them called "This Is America." To be honest, as much as I love to talk, I don't really love to have a video camera in my face. I was a little bit nervous, but I went anyway. Part of my discussion with the host Dennis Wholey centered on the word "good." I asked Dennis, "What does good look like?"

During the interview I was talking to Dennis about something I had seen on Oprah. Oprah had a TV special about the girls' school that she built in Africa. They filmed her talking with the girls, and every time she said to one of them, "You are such a good girl, you are such a good girl!" I found myself shouting at Oprah through the television, "What is *good*? Don't you remember how to Speak the Language of the Virtues?" How more meaningful it would have been had she said to the girls, "Wow, you have such courage and determination getting up so early and walking in such a dangerous neighborhood to get to school each day."

After my interview with Dennis was over I took the subway home. As I replayed the interview in my head, I began to "beat myself up. " I was allowing "The Committee" in my head to take over. You know that committee. It's the part of our ego that gathers and spews out all the self-deprecating criticism and negativity. My committee was going full throttle, telling me, *You are so stupid; I can't believe you "dissed" Oprah on TV! And then you made those little "puppy dog" sounds when you were talking about how complimenting or praising kids begets more praise! You are going to get in so much trouble!* It went on and on for the entire ride that lasted 45 minutes.

But something happened as soon as I got home. I walked through my house and sat down on the back porch. I looked up into the sky and had a 180 degree shift. I thought to myself, *Oh my goodness, you had a lot of courage to be on national television for the founders! You sure showed a lot of enthusiasm in the way you were talking about The Virtues Project. Though you probably could have been a little more tactful and used some self-discipline when you were talking about Oprah!*

It was at that moment, three years into The Virtues Project, when I realized that using the language was a *choice*. I realized that I could also acknowledge myself and use the language to guide and correct myself instead of beating myself up.

How did I learn the language? One way is by doing a virtues pick every day. The virtue I pick is either an affirmation or an invitation. When I read the practice of the virtue on the back of a card, I turn each statement around as a question and ask myself, *Am I exhibiting these behaviors? If not, what can I do in order to exhibit these behaviors?*

Another way I have been practicing the language is through emails. In the beginning when I was learning the language, it was easier for me to do it electronically because I could take some time to think about the virtue that I wanted to acknowledge, as well as the evidence. I reread my emails so I could make sure that they sounded the way I wanted them to sound, especially because things can be misinterpreted so easily through emails. I also attached a virtues card to each email. For example, if I signed the email "with gratitude," I would include the gratitude card. It was inspiring to see the positive responses I got when I included a virtues card.

Learning to Speak the Language of Virtues is like learning a new language. It's much like going back to high school or middle school when you first learned another language or even like coming from another country and learning the native language. At first it is awkward and hard; it did not come naturally. It took a lot of practice, right? There were things that you did to make it easier for yourself. Perhaps you wrote down key phrases and memorized those, and you used those key phrases over and over again until you mastered them and were ready to increase your vocabulary. Once you mastered the basics, the language became more natural over time. Learning to Speak the Language of the Virtues follows a very similar process.

At first, Speaking the Language of Virtues might feel unnatural and contrived. You might think to yourself as I did, *In order to learn this language do I have to use these virtue cards as flash cards?* No, just be gentle with yourself and make a commitment to do a virtues pick every day.

The virtues cards and the language are really powerful, especially when you are having parent/teacher conferences or when you are writing comments on your students' report cards. Looking at your students through the lens of virtues is really powerful. It affirms or invites those character qualities and the example they represent.

Speaking the Language of Virtues calls for the use of three parts:
- **The stem** - an opening phrase that acknowledges or invites someone to a virtue
- **The virtue** - a positive character quality
- **The evidence** - how the virtue is being demonstrated

If you say, "I see your determination," "I see your" is the stem and "determination" is the virtue. However, the evidence is missing. The student may not understand what it was that he/ she demonstrated that showed determination.

If you say, "You really worked through that hard problem without giving up," the student knows he or she is capable of working through that problem but they may not realize that working hard "without giving up" is the virtue of determina-tion. When we use the language, the virtue and the evidence together, then the virtue becomes a transferrable skill.

About four years into using the Language of the Virtues my son said to me, "Mom, just speak normal, speak the old way." I was devastated. I couldn't understand how this young man who helps me when I have a Virtues Project booth at trade shows and is really enthusiastic about The Virtues Project suddenly wanted me to stop Speaking the Language. Being respectful of his wishes I stopped...for all of about two hours. My son was downstairs and I was upstairs. I don't think I really said much to him, maybe something like, "Please put the laundry in the dryer" instead of "Please be helpful and put the laundry in the dryer." A couple hours after he told me to speak "the old way" he said, "OK, OK, Mom, Speak the Language of the Virtues." And that was that. I guess he just needed to be reminded of how different it feels.

Remember the committee I spoke about on the subway ride home after my interview? If you have ever wanted a way to "fire" that committee and welcome a new, positive one, I would encourage you to try the following process.

First, read and commit to believing the following statement: "Dear Committee, thank you for your loyalty and generosity of time, shaming and blaming me all these years. I will no longer need your services and would appreciate it if you would please leave forever. Thank you for your cooperation, good-bye."

Now it's time to replace them with a new committee. What might comprise that committee? Where might you find it? The new committee has always been with you. The new committee is made up of your virtues. Take a moment to raise the virtues into your consciousness and make this commitment to yourself:

"Dear New Committee, thank you for your patience and perseverance being with me all these years. I realize I may not have always been mindful that you were there. However, I make the commitment to be more purposeful in using you all, not only when speaking to others but also when speaking to myself. Thank you for your service and your commitment to supporting me always. Welcome home."

How does it feel to know that you can be gentle with yourself? Next time you forget the papers you stayed up all night grading on the kitchen table, instead of saying to yourself, "Oh my goodness, I am so stupid, I can't believe I left the students' papers on the kitchen table," you can say, "It would be helpful for me to be more orderly and put the papers in my backpack before going to sleep."

The Power of our Words

We have all heard the adage "*Sticks and stones can break my bones but words can never hurt me.*" But if we think about this, is it really true? It is words, especially when spoken by people that we care about most, which can really have a profound effect on us. This is especially true when we are young.

Think about when you were younger. Did someone you love and trust, perhaps a parent or teacher, ever say something to you that made you think you were not loveable or not valued? Maybe a teacher said you were a bad little boy or girl. Maybe they called you a bully when they told you to stop hitting the person next to you. How does that help shape your identity? If someone you trust calls you a bully when you are younger, perhaps you grow up to become a bully; it becomes a self-fulfilling prophecy. Maybe your caregivers never taught you how to show your feelings in a kinder, gentler way. On the other hand, if they called you a baby and weakling, perhaps you grew up doubting your own strength and now allow people to take advantage of you.

When we use the power of the language to positively guide people to a certain behavior, we are using that character strength and the evidence. Then that child or adult knows that they are capable of exhibiting a particular virtue and that it is a choice. Again, it goes back to Carol Dweck's work about a growth mindset.

Sticks and stones can break my bones but words can break my spirit... that's really how that is. But we can also flip it around to the positive. *Sticks and stones can break my bones and words can give me strength to move through it.*

In the chapter entitled "Purifying the Language of Our Life" from Linda Kavelin-Popov's book *A Pace of Grace – Virtues for a Sustainable Life*, she writes about replacing negativity with virtues. She talks about replacing the four Cs of contempt, contention, control and criticism with the three As of acceptance, appreciation and assertiveness.

Linda writes, "Acceptance is seeing each person as whole, noticing the virtues the person does have, giving up the desire to control and change them and instead entering into a loving relationship with them as they are. Appreciation is feeling and expressing positive regard and gratitude for one another's nature and actions, both what we are and what we do. Assertiveness is asking for what we need in a respectful and peaceful way, setting clear boundaries and telling the truth as we see it about what is just.

"When we replace the negativity with these three As it really helps the person we are interacting with to become open to having a more loving and cooperative relationship." Take a minute to think about the three As in the different areas of your life: at home with your family and at work with your colleagues and your students. Consider how they can make a difference.

In Jennifer Abrams book *Having Hard Conversations*, she writes about the importance of scripting your initial comments where you are going to have a courageous conversation with a colleague. She makes some excellent points about the different steps to follow: setting the tone and the purpose of the conversation; getting to the point and naming it professionally; giving examples; describing the effect of this behavior on the school, colleagues or students; and sharing your willingness to resolve the issue and have a dialog or discussion.

When you use the Language of Virtues, the person you are having the conversation with will be that much more open to hearing what you have to say. The chance of them putting up walls is much less likely to happen.

In Robert Sutton's book *The No Asshole Rule*, he writes about the assumptions in the language we use; the lens we see the world through can have a significant impact on how we treat others. Even seemingly small differences in language that we hear and use can determine whether we cooperate or compete.

There is a great deal of research about bullying in schools and the work place, as well as the effects of a positive attitude that lead to positive performances. In *The No Asshole Rule*, Sutton talks about people who persistently leave others feeling de-energized and undermine their own performance by turning coworkers and bosses against them and stifling motivation throughout their social networks.

Sutton and his colleagues found that being an "energizer" was one of the strongest influences for positive performance evaluations. The strategy consultants were especially prone to giving lower evaluations to the "de-energizers" in their ranks.

What is a quick way to help to energize your colleagues or your kids? It is to acknowledge them. When you see them exhibiting a virtue, give them an acknowledgment. You will instantly notice how their faces light up, how they sit up taller in their chairs and how they have more energy and enthusiasm to do what you have asked of them.

In the book *How Full is Your Bucket* by Tom Rath and Donald Clifton, they describe how we communicate with one another as either a drop in or a drip out of someone's bucket. When we give an acknowledgment, we are helping to add to a person's sense of self, their sense of purpose. We keep it positive and we fill the bucket with drops, which allows the person to be better equipped to be of service to others. On the other hand, when we say or do unkind things it is a drip and the bucket is actually empting out. When you are running on low energy and low acknowledgements, it is harder for you to have the power to be kind and supportive toward one another or to do your best job.

Virtuous Vibrations

When we are kind to others, it is like paying forward the kindnesses done to us. For example, when we are courteous and hold the door open for somebody or are kind and give someone an acknowledgment, it makes them feel better and raises their "vibration." The vibration is energetic frequencies that can help you feel positive and happy, or negative and unhappy. As a result of those positive interactions, they are likely to pass on and continue to move the positive energy forward. On the other hand, if somebody says something hurtful, cuts somebody off in traffic or flashes an unkind hand gesture, that could cause a negativity spiral. A person on the receiving end of negative energy will likely pass the negativity onto someone else.

Dr. David Hawkins, a healing psychologist who uses theoretical concepts from particle physics, nonlinear dynamics, and chaos theory to support his study of human behavior, has created a "Scale of Levels of Consciousness" in his book *Power vs Force*. Looking at his map of consciousness reveals different virtues that are calibrated at different vibrations, or levels of energy. For example, "Courage" is neutral and calibrates at 200. On the other hand "Pride," "Anger," "Desire," "Fear," "Grief," "Apathy," "Guilt," "Shame" and "Humiliation" are emotions that vibrate at the lowest frequencies between zero and 200. When you come from those low vibrations you are coming from a place of force, a place of push back and negativity. Coming from a place of force almost always results in meeting resistance.

Vibrating at between 250 and 1,000 calibrations means you are coming from a place of power; it is empowering for others to be around you. "Trust," "Optimism," "Forgiveness," "Understanding," "Reverence," "Serenity" and "Bliss" are high vibration emotions. These positive emotions can give you power and empower others.

Going back to Carol Dweck's work, if we look at the map of consciousness, the fixed mindset would register at the lower end of the vibrations, and the growth mindset would be those calibrating at the high end, above "Courage." Attribution Retraining can help move others from a fixed mindset to growth mindset, from a place of force to a place of power. Attribution Retraining can help replace a student's unhelpful explanations about his or her academic performance with explanations and strategies that will sustain his or her motivation to move toward success.

When I demonstrate this energetic principle in my workshops, I ask my participants to think about whether they believe that language can inspire or discourage. Then I show them pictures of water crystals taken by the Japanese water researcher Dr. Masaru Emoto. In his research, Dr. Emoto put labels on water bottles with positive words such as "love and gratitude" and negative words such as "you make me sick." Then he froze the water and looked at the water crystals under a special microscope. He found that the water crystals that had positive words on them crystalized beautifully and looked like diamonds. The ones that had negative words were murky and muddy. Dr. Emoto believes that human consciousness has an effect on the molecular structure of water.

Now consider how this relates to us. We, and the world around us, are primarily made up of water. I demonstrate the connection between the power and effect of language and the energetic principles David Hawkins describes and Dr. Emoto illuminates, by using the applied muscle testing technique, or applied kinesiology. This is a sure way to help skeptics experience this first-hand.

I ask a courageous volunteer to come and raise their dominant arm straight out to their side. I ask them to tell me their name to get a "baseline" of their strength. While they are telling me their real name, I place two of my fingers right above their wrist and push down on their arm while they resist. Because they are coming from a place of truth their arm stays strong and does not lower. When you are in your truth, you are stronger. Then I ask them to tell me a name that is not theirs, to lie to me. Now, when I push down with two fingers above their wrist, as they resist, their arm goes down.

We go through this same process with the words and phrases: "hate," "love," "do it" and "let's do it" in this order. More often than not, "hate" and "do it" make their arm go down;

the participants cannot keep their arm up; but with "love" and "let's do it" they stay strong.

Let's think about it for a minute. "Love" and "hate" are pretty easy. "Hate" is easily recognized as a negative word. "Love" makes you stronger because it is positive, a high vibration word. But what about "do it" and "let's do it?" "Do it" is a command. When we come from a place of force, we meet resistance. "Let's do it" is actually the virtue of unity and cooperation. It is a high frequency phrase, and it invites strength.

I encourage you to look up Dr. Emoto's work, *The Hidden Messages in Water* as well as David Hawkins' series, especially *Power vs Force.*

Language Shapes Our Beliefs

One of my favorite authors and researchers is Eric Jensen. In his book *Brain Based Learning* he writes about "when authority figures of any kind make a statement about a child, the child is likely to accept it as true. Whether it is close to the truth or it is far away from it as the moon, children do not have the brain development for reasoning until about the age of ten or 12.

"By this time they have built up a whole set of capability beliefs many of them erroneously, that are already shaping their future. A capability belief is likely to be formed when even a well-meaning parent, relative or teacher blurts out in a moment of frustration, 'why don't you understand this simple concept,' or worse, 'you will never learn what you need to at this rate.'"

"Such false statements serve as a catalyst for many poor attitudes and their impact can be a lifetime of learning paralysis."

In Daniel Pink's book *Drive,* he talks about the differences among a compliment, praise and acknowledgment. A compliment is something like "That's a pretty picture." or "You have a nice smile." Praise is something like "Good job." Both of those are extrinsic motivators. Often times when we give a compliment somebody might think, "Oh, she does not mean it, she's just trying to make me feel good." There is no evidence to support the compliment or praise, and in fact it can create some cognitive dissonance that may do more damage than good.

Praise can create the wanting for more external praise and pats on the back, and may prevent people from developing their own intrinsic motivation. This can be seen in schools that focus solely on the use of coupons as rewards for positive behavior under PBIS (Positive Behavioral Interventions and Support).

Virtues acknowledgments include the critical component of evidence to show how someone is demonstrating a virtue, and therefore helps the individual internalize the virtue.

Pink also writes about money as a motivator when we are doing menial tasks. However, it is really mastery and meaning that drives us to do what we do in most circumstances.

One of my friends and a well-loved educator is Hal Urban. He is the author of *Life's Great Lessons* and *Positive Words, Powerful Results – Simple Ways to Honor, Affirm and Celebrate Life*, as well as many other books. In *Positive Words* he has great activities that you can do with students to help them see the power of their words.

In one activity Hal gives students a list of words such as "destroy," "jail," "suffer," "hate" and "damage." He asks students to think about what kind of feelings come to mind with these words. He gives the kids a few minutes to read the words and talk about them and as expected, they are feeling pretty "yucky" after reading those words. Then he gives them another sheet of paper with the words "love," "friend," "kindness," "peace," "forgive" and "joy." He then asks the students to think about what kind of feelings come to mind with these words. As expected students say they feel really "great."

If you ask the students to use the two different lists to write sentences, you will probably get positive statements using the positive words and negative statements using the negative words. When he gave out the list of negative words he noticed that there was a lot of tension in the room. When he gave out the positive words he noticed that actually their spirits were raised. This is just one more tangible example of how language affects us.

Something that I learned in Alanon, a 12-step program for families of alcoholics, was to think before we speak and ask ourselves if what we are about to say is kind, true, and necessary, and if it is necessary, then does it need to be said now? If we can ask ourselves those questions and package our responses through the filter of virtues and the virtues language, it will undoubtedly be received in a much more positive way.

From Possibilities to Probabilities

One of my favorite books is *The Art of Possibility* by Rosemary Zander and Ben Zander. I first found out about this book when I was studying for my Masters in Education, Media Design and Technology. I took this book with me to Miami when I went to the YPO conference. I planned to read it on my trip back home. My brother saw it and he said, "Hey, I tried to get Ben Zander to come talk to my group but he wasn't available." I thought *Cool, we have an author we both like.*

At the end of that conference, my brother and I were sitting in the auditorium with about 3,000 people, and up on the screen it said "Possibilities." We looked at each other and said, "What are the chances?" Then out from behind the curtain walked Ben Zander.

As if that wasn't coincidence enough, at the same time I got a text from one of my traveling laptop sisters, Susan, a friend from my Masters Program... who wrote, "Dara, did you start reading *The Art of Possibility*? It is all about what you are about."

Here was Ben Zander, standing in front of me. There I was holding his book. And a friend was texting me about it. It was a powerful moment. Clearly I needed to read this book, and I did. There were many profound things that stood out for me.

I think one of my favorite chapters was about "Giving Everybody an A." He explains that you start from the place of expectation that there is inherent nobility in all of our students, and they are all capable.

In his book, Zander lets his class know that everybody is starting out with an A. "Their responsibility is to write [him] a letter and postdate it for the end of the semester as if they have already completed the class. In their letter they are to spell out what they have done in order to earn that A."

It is about setting intentions, about being mindful, and thinking about the virtues that they are going to need to call on in order to be successful. What he found was when he started with that activity and the kids really knew what it was they needed to do and take responsibility for their own success, that more often than not those kids really did earn an A.

I can relate to this personally. In high school and as an undergraduate at the University of Maryland, I was a bit like Bart Simpson, the classic underachiever. I was the class skipper (not such a great reputation for an up and coming teacher to have) but that was my MO (method of operation). I was one of those kids who got into trouble a lot for talking too much in class. In sixth grade I remember sitting next to my teacher Mrs. Marlette and writing notes and throwing them to my classmates--pretty disrespectful behavior. I am so sorry Mrs. Marlette for being so disrespectful. I certainly was attention-seeking, and didn't know how to ask for it in a positive way. Most teachers have students like me in their classes. Perhaps you were one of them?

My teachers used to tell me that I needed to be more respectful, and needed to have more self-discipline, but they never taught me what respect and self-discipline looked like. I was never taught how to call on self-discipline in order to be more respectful.

When I was working on my Masters degree, our syllabus for each class would be released on Monday mornings at 12:30 am. We often had only a couple of days to have a full project completed and a 500-page book read. One night around 10:30 pm I was sitting at my computer, exhausted, and I remember saying to myself, *I am not going to do my homework tonight; I am just going to check my email.*

Then those darn virtues started creeping into my thoughts. I needed to be reliable to my teammates, so I needed to finish my part of an assignment. When I didn't feel like writing a citation, I did it anyway because of the virtues of integrity and trustworthiness. When I wanted to rush through an assignment and cut corners, the virtue of excellence would fly into my brain. If you looked into my office window in the middle of the night, you could see me taking my elbows and pushing back as if I was literally pushing those virtues and telling them to go away! Fortunately, they did not leave me alone.

As a result of learning and developing the virtues and knowing that they were transferrable skills, I ended up earning a 4.0 and three different awards from my professors. Again, I experienced how these virtues were a choice. Once I practiced them and really understood their benefits, I was able to put them into use. They genuinely transformed my life. If I could begin to embrace my virtues at almost 50, then you know it is never too late to begin this awareness.

I would like to invite you to make a commitment to do a virtues pick every day. Write virtues vouchers or just include them in your emails as ways to acknowledge others for the virtues that you see in them. If you keep a journal I invite you to write about how you demonstrate your virtues each day. Take time to reflect on your actions. If you did something that you were not particularly proud of, invite yourself to demonstrate a specific virtue and how that might change the outcome in the future. I promise, if you commit to Speaking the Language of the Virtues, it won't just change your language, it will change your life and the lives of everyone you connect with.

Respect

Respect is an attitude of honoring ourselves and others as people of value. We care for each person's dignity. Everyone has the right to expect respect. We show respect in the courtesy of our words, and in our tone of voice. We are all exquisitely sensitive to respect. When we treat others as we would like to be treated, we raise the level of trust and peace in our relationships. Respect is having reverence for the earth and all living things. When we live respectfully, we are a source of grace in the world.

The Virtues Project™

1 What kind of "self talk" do you usually use? Is it positive and supportive or negative and self-deprecating?
2 When do you have a growth mindset and when is it fixed?
3 What do you say and do to encourage your students to have a growth mindset?

Chapter Six

Lovin' the Learning: Recognizing Teachable Moments

"In all situations, it is my response that decides whether a crisis will be escalated or de-escalated and a child humanized or de-humanized."
Haim Ginott

Life is for Learning Lessons

I believe that everything does happen for a reason, and that life is for learning our lessons. When lessons that are painful occur, it is an opportunity to get curious, not furious, and find the gift.

When my kids were younger I was given a book called *The Blessing of a Skinned Knee* by Dr. Wendy Mogul. It uses Jewish teachings to raise self-reliant children. I was one of those moms who, if left unchecked, would probably have been a helicopter mom today. For example, if one of my little ones would fall down I might immediately run, pick them up and ask, "Are you ok, are you ok, are you ok?" Unfortunately that would have fed into their learned helplessness.

What I learned from reading *The Blessing of a Skinned Knee* is that when kids are little and they fall down, we need to give them the opportunity to get up by themselves. When kids are little there are always little problems that arise; if they fall down and then stand up by themselves, they realize that they are strong and capable, and that they can be self-reliant.

As children get older and problems appear to be larger, the same principle applies. If they can work it out themselves, let them. When possible, be open to allowing natural consequences to play out. For example, if one of your children forgets to bring her homework to school, don't rush to the school and drop the homework off for her. Instead, talk with her about what happened. Help her identify the virtue that was missing that caused her to forget her homework and help her develop a strategy for strengthening that virtue. If the reason was due to a lack of orderliness, have the student embrace this as a Teachable Moment and work with her on a plan for putting her homework in a place where she will remember it. If we are always bailing them out, then our kids will never learn their lessons.

In The Virtues Project, part of the strategy of Recognizing Teachable Moments is the ability to rename a negative trait and reframe it as a virtue. In Dr. Mogul's book, she uses a similar exercise where she asks you to think of your child's worst trait, the little habit or attitude that really gets on your nerves. Or that medium size habit that your child's teacher keeps bringing up at a parent conference. Or the really big one that wakes you up at three o'clock in the morning with frightening visions of your little guy all grown up and living on the streets alone and addicted to heroin. Dr. Mogul uses this as an icebreaker where she asks participants to nod their heads when they have come up with an example. (Are you nodding your head? How could you not be?) She lets participants know that if they were able to come up with their child's worst trait, they now know their child's greatest strength. It is hidden in his "worst quality" just waiting to be let out.

During a Virtues Project workshop, we ask the same type of question: "What behavior pushes your buttons the most?" My son's stubbornness is always the first thing to come to my mind. Oh my goodness, he is so incredibly stubborn! When he wants something, he goes after it until he gets it. His stubbornness is actually one of his greatest gifts! When we reframe and rename stubbornness it is actually the virtue of determination.

I have seen that virtue of determination show up in positive ways for him. When he was working through his different belts in karate, it gave him the strength to keep going. Another time he wanted to transfer to a particular university and, through his determination, was accepted within two weeks of applying. Now he is grown up and wants to become a doctor. I know that determination is going to help him achieve his goals.

Recognizing Teachable Moments is not just about helping others to see how what they are doing can be done differently. It is also about checking our own integrity--about "walking our talk." In Coach John Wooden's book, *Wooden: A Lifetime of Observations and Reflections On and Off the Court*, he talks about being a good example, and how powerful that is as a teaching device. The quote below is one of my favorites from his book.

> *"No written word or spoken plea can teach our youth*
> *what they should be.*
> *Nor all the books on all the shelves,*
> *it's what the teachers are themselves."*
>
> *Author Unknown*

If we think about this for a moment, when we are teaching our kids to be respectful, are we doing it in a respectful way? When we want them to be reliable and show up on time, do we pick them up from the playground on time? If we ask them to be orderly and put their belongings neatly in their desks, do our desks model orderliness? This is something very important; we need to walk our talk.

It is not so much about what we say but what we do. It is helpful to remember the old adage, "Your actions speak so loudly I can't hear what you are saying." This adage reminds me of a video that educators at Fox High School created called, "The List." "The List" compares the behaviors of bullies and educators. Read over the lists carefully. Take a moment to reflect. When are you a bully and when are you an educator?

Bullies-Educators: Which One Are You?

Bullies	Educators
• Bullies exert their own control.	• Educators teach self-control.
• Bullies use sarcasm to turn disruptions into confrontations.	• Educators diffuse minor situations with humor.
• Bullies compare children to one another.	• Educators see each student's uniqueness.
• Bullies punish students for being unsuccessful.	• Educators help all students feel successful.
• Bullies humiliate.	• Educators educate.
• Bullies let students know who's boss.	• Educators let students know they care.
• Bullies are judgmental.	• Educators are judicious.
• Bullies are reactive; they blame students for the lack of order in their classrooms.	• Educators are proactive; they create classroom environments that foster good behavior.

What Is the Gift?

In the book *Teaching and Joy* edited by Robert Sornson and James Scott, one of the stories I really appreciated was an interview with Dr. Bernie Segal, the author of *Why Bad Things Happen to Good People*. When he was being interviewed, Sornson asked Dr. Segal, "If you were a new parent today and could start all over again knowing all that you have been able to gather in this life, what would you teach your children?"

Segal responded, "If I were a parent today I would touch my child often because that lets children know that they are loved and it also changes them physically. I would repeat 'I love you' to that child. I would instill discipline, not punishment. I would also keep saying to that child that I am not perfect as a parent. I have never had lessons so if something comes up and I am not doing it right, help me out or forgive me.

"When problems occur I would also say to the child what my mother used to say to me, 'God is redirecting you, something good will come of this.' As Norman Vincent Peale's mother used to say to him, 'Norman, if God slams one door, further down the corridor another will open.'"

Segal goes on to say that whether it is something perceived as positive or something perceived as negative, it is helpful for us to ask the question, "What can I do with this? What is the lesson in it?"

That is the gist of Recognizing Teachable Moments. It is looking at the lesson, the gift, the test, or whatever comes up and saying, "What is the learning? What virtues do I need or get to strengthen?"

Another story that illuminates what Dr. Segal is talking about is a parable that was turned into a children's book called *The Little Soul and the Sun* by Neal Donald Walsch. I heard this story a week after my ex-husband and father of my two children passed away from alcoholism. At the time of his death, Jim was a homeless alcoholic. I had exhausted all possibilities of trying to help him get sober. As a result of his alcoholism and the pain Jim's drinking brought to our family, I was introduced to Al-Anon, a 12-Step Program for families of alcoholics.

The following information is taken from the Al-Anon website (www.al-anon.alateen.org/): "The Al-Anon Family Groups are a fellowship of relatives and friends of alcoholics who share their experience, strength, and hope, in order to solve their common problems. We believe alcoholism is a family illness, and that changed attitudes can aid recovery.

"We who live, or have lived, with the problem of alcoholism understand as perhaps few others can. We, too, were lonely and frustrated, but in Al-Anon we discover that no situation is really hopeless and that it is possible for us to find contentment, and even happiness, whether the alcoholic is still drinking or not.

"We urge you to try our program. It has helped many of us find solutions that lead to serenity. So much depends on our own attitudes, and as we learn to place our problem in its true perspective, we find it loses its power to dominate our thoughts and our lives."

If you can relate to any of these feelings, I encourage you to visit the Al-Anon website and find a meeting in your area.

I had been going to Al-Anon for about 15 years at the time of Jim's death and had a strong belief that things happen for a reason. But it really was not until *The Little Soul and the Sun* was read to me that I understood the whole sacrifice that my ex-husband had made in order to help the kids and I learn the lessons that we needed to learn.

The story goes like this... There is a Little Soul and he is talking to God (Good Orderly Direction, Great Out Doors, the Great Universe, Spirit, Higher Power, use whatever works for you). The Little Soul says, "I want to know what I am." God says to him, "You are the light." The Little Soul says, "No, no, no, no. I want to know what I am." And he goes back and forth with God. Finally, God says, "You are the light," and he starts listing the virtues such as Love, Kindness, Patience, Tolerance, Forgiveness and more.

The Little Soul says, "I know, I want to know what it is like to be Forgiveness." And God says, "Oh my." Then a Second Little Soul steps forward and says, "I will come into the next lifetime and I will help you to be Forgiveness. But I may have to lower my vibration so much that I may not recognize myself and you may not recognize me because I might do something so heinous." The First Little Soul says, "Why would you do that?" And the Second Little Soul says, "Because I love you that much and you've done that for me."

Having heard that story I realized that Jim was not a bad guy; I knew he wasn't. I knew that alcoholism was a disease and that he had taken the hard life to help the kids and me understand what Forgiveness is all about and to help us find a spiritual path so that our lives would have more joy, meaning and purpose.

When I returned home from the mentorship, I shared the story with my kids, who were 13 and almost 16 at the time. It was very healing for them as well, and it helped them to understand that things really do happen for a reason. I am forever grateful to Jim for helping us learn the lesson of Forgiveness. I am also grateful to Wendy, Barb and Renee, the wonderful women who

read that story to me at such an opportune time of learning…
quite the Teachable Moment.

For years I have just been awed by the beautiful writings
and the wisdom of Mattie Stepanek. Unfortunately, Mattie
passed away several years ago from muscular dystrophy. His
three siblings had also passed away before him. God bless his
mother, Jeni. She is such a strong woman and has such a great
positive outlook on life. I know for sure that is where Mattie got
his strength, in addition to his deep faith in God.

*One of the poems that Mattie wrote in 2000 is called "Choice
Lessons" and it goes like this:*

Choice Lessons
By Mattie J. T. Stepanek

Growth brings change.
Unpredictable change,
Which can bring
Hesitancy to optimism.
It is essential that we cope
With the realities of the past
And the uncertainties of the future
With a pure and chosen hope.
Not a blind faith,
But a strengthened choice.
Then, we can have the
Fortitude and wisdom necessary
To integrate life's many lessons
That collect beyond points and time.
Growing like this will help
Build a good future,
For individuals
For communities,
And for the world.

What a beautiful way to illuminate how virtues can help us
recognize Teachable Moments.

It's All Good

It really is "all good." *In Discipline with Dignity, New Challenges for New Solutions* by Richard L. Curwin, Alan M. Mendler and Brian D. Mendler, the authors have a great definition of "reframing." They explain that reframing is "the skill of understanding a situation in a way that gives us the best chance for a positive outcome."

It is not about making excuses for, or ignoring behavior; how we behave will depend on whether we see a student as "strong-willed" or "stubborn." This goes along with the renaming and reframing. Instead of saying that somebody is stubborn, look beneath that stubbornness and look at it in a positive light and recognize the virtue of stubbornness is really determination.

We can leverage a student's strength by saying, "Wow, I notice that you never give up. You have such determination. You never quit. You keep working hard, even when things get tough." vs. "You are so stubborn. When are you just going to give it all up? We need to move on!"

When we acknowledge somebody's strength and use it as a virtue, they know they have that virtue in them. They recognize that calling on that virtue is a choice and they can use it in a positive way.

Consider some regular examples that happen every day in the life of a classroom. How often have you heard yourself saying, "How many times have I told you guys to clean up this mess?" or "Please stop your talking and get back to work." or "Really, I can't believe you forgot your homework again."

What if we were to actually guide the students back to a certain virtue and say this instead: "Ok everybody, please be orderly and remember to put your papers neatly in your folder and put your folders in your backpacks." We might also say, "Thank you for your cooperation and orderliness in hanging your backpacks up on the hooks and putting your jackets on top of them." This lets the students know what orderliness looks like. It guides that towards success.

When we want students to stop talking and get back to work, we can call students to the virtue of purposefulness and say: "All right boys and girls, please be purposeful and finish your assignment, let's save the talking for recess."

Finally, with the homework example we can say: "What will help you to be responsible and bring your homework to class each day?"

Another way to Recognize Teachable Moments is by using an "Act with Tact Positivity Sandwich." It is basically giving a virtues acknowledgement, acknowledging what the strength virtue is in a particular situation; and then inviting that person to a growth virtue and conclude by thanking them.

For example, if a student is rushing through her work, working quickly so she can get it all done before the class ends, she is being purposeful, but not being diligent and doing her best work. Instead of handing it back and saying, "I know you can do this neater, do it again," you can acknowledge her and say, "I really see your purposefulness in the way that you have made sure that you get all of your work done by the end of class. Please be diligent and slow down and do your very best work without rushing. Thank you for your commitment to doing your best work each day." Can't you just feel the difference? Imagine how your students (colleagues, family members, etc...) will feel when you commit to using this type of authentic and meaningful feedback.

Stabilization

Sometimes in the heat of the moment, instead of reframing, we need to take one step back to get into "Stabilization." In *Discipline with Dignity*, authors Richard Curwin and Allen Mendler give examples of "Stabilization" in terms of when "...emergency room doctors, police officers, firefighters and more all know how dangerous it is to go forward in an unstable situation. They have to stop the bleeding, stop the bombing or do whatever it takes before the healing process can begin."

The same is true in the classroom. If a student is really upset and says, "This school really sucks." Then the teacher can say, "Are you telling me how you really feel?" If the student says, "Yes," then we can acknowledge her for her honesty. When you know where a person is coming from, and you allow that person to be seen and heard, it helps to deescalate and stabilize the behavior. Then we can reframe and rename what is going on with the individual and call him/her back to the virtue.

Commanders vs Loving Guides and Facilitators

Another wonderful resource is a book called *Managing Your Classroom with Heart – A Guide to Nourishing Adolescent Learners* by Katie Ridnouer. She includes a great survey where she asks a series of six questions:

- Can you learn from a teacher you dislike, why or why not?
- How did a teacher you disliked make you feel about yourself?
- Describe a teacher you dislike, no names please.
- Can you learn from a teacher you care about, why or why not?
- How did a teacher you care about make you feel about yourself?
- Describe a teacher you care about.

I do believe that if we read these questions and reflect on them as educators that they will provide some insightful, Teachable Moments for us. Do we recognize our own Teachable Moments? Do we run our classrooms as if we are commanders (as Katie used to run her classroom) or as loving guides and facilitators, making it easy for students to learn not just the curriculum that is handed to us but the curriculum of life?

On the path to Recognizing Teachable Moments, Linda Kavelin-Popov asks a really powerful question in *A Pace of Grace: Virtues for a Sustainable Life*. "How does it feel when you are being led by your soul vs. driven by your ego?"

How quickly and easily can we as educators get amnesia? Let's face it, the demands of a classroom are pretty intense. We have so much going on all at once and the curriculum is so demanding. We have students with multiple learning styles, and they all have different skills, interests and issues to support. We are expected to differentiate, yet make sure to hit all of the outcomes in the ever-changing curriculum. In our commitment to fulfill all of our responsibilities, sometimes fear can creep in. As we say in 12-Step meetings, "Fear is actually an acronym for "False Evidence Appearing Real." It can allow us to forget the reason we went into education to begin with. It is not just about individual outcomes, but it is also about creating whole, caring young people who can be thriving, contributing members of our society. In that ego-driven "fear space," we can get scared, our tempers can flare and we can say things that we later regret.

However, when we can remember to come from a place of trust, by doing the footwork, building relationships with our students, preparing our lesson plans, continuing professional development to build our own capacity, then we are able to be "led by our souls." We can trust that once we have prepared to the best of our ability we can turn the rest over and be fully present for those Teachable Moments that arise on a regular basis. Surely there will be enough time for what is truly important, for what really matters.

How Do You Define Success?

As you can probably tell, one of my favorite educators and someone whom I admire deeply (and actually had the honor of talking to once on the telephone), is Coach John Wooden. He is a hero of both my brother and me. One day I was in the children's section of a book store and was skimming through a book called *Inch and Miles*. Because of the title, I thought it had to do with math. As I was going through the book I started seeing adorable illustrations with words in large print like "enthusiasm," "self-discipline," "loyalty," "cooperation" and other character qualities. I thought to myself, *This reminds me a lot of Coach John Wooden's Success Pyramid.* When I got to the end of the book, there it was: The Success Pyramid for Kids. Given that I am really committed to getting The Virtues Project out there in the world, I thought, *Who better than to connect with but Coach?*

I decided to send him an email, and got a response back from his partner Steve Jamison. After some "back and forth" communications, we talked on the telephone and Steve gave me Coach's number. He also gave me some guidance on what to say.

So I called Coach up, expecting to get his answering machine and leave him a message. When he picked up the phone I was really startled and I said, "Uhhhhhh, hi Coach, how are you?" And he answered, "Better than any 87-year-old has the right to be."

I got to have a quick conversation with him and acknowledge his commitment to excellence and all that he has given, not just to the world in terms of basketball, but in terms of what commitment, passion and excellence look like. He told me that one of the reasons he wrote the book *Inch and Miles* was because his granddaughter is a kindergarten teacher. At the time Coach and I spoke, I was a kindergarten teacher as well.

It was incredibly inspiring to have a conversation with this great man who epitomized humility, integrity and excellence. As educators, we are confronted with challenges on a daily basis. When those challenges arise, do we meet them from a place of integrity? Do we choose to have the courage to be who we truly are, or do we give in to what other people want and expect from us?

About 12 years ago I was given my first book by Coach that he co-authored with Steve Jamison called *Wooden – A Lifetime of Observations and Reflections On and Off the Court*. I was given this book, inscribed with beautiful messages, from several of my Apple Distinguished Educator colleagues. At that time we were on UCLA's campus for three weeks doing technology integration workshops for teachers. One afternoon I was facilitating a workshop. In the middle of this workshop, out of the blue, a man raised his hand and when I called on him he said, "Quit being so fake. How can you be so happy all the time? You are just putting on an act." It threw me off guard; I took a deep breath, I looked around the room at 300 faces staring back and me. I don't remember exactly what I said to him, however it went something like this, "Actually, this is who I am and I have a lot to be grateful for, and that is why I am really happy."

After the workshop several of the people rushed up to me and said, "Oh man what a jerk. Are you ok?" I let them know I was fine and that what this gentleman thought of me was none of my business. I felt sincerely grateful that I teach from a place of joy. Sometimes when we have integrity and are "walking our talk" it can push the buttons of people who are perhaps not being true to themselves. It takes strength, determination and detachment to keep going down that path.

When we stand before our class, or stand next to one of our students or the parents we work with, when we can be true, authentic, and come from a place of love and integrity, we have what is most important. We do not have to have all the answers, we do not have to "put on airs" and pretend we are better or know it all; we just need to come from that place of truth. That is what our students most need from us. They need us to be individual heroes who, as our own personal leaders on our personal paths can model what dignity and integrity looks like for them.

In the book *365 Meditations for Teachers* by Greg Henry Quinn, his reading for September 9th is: "Compassion transcends ego. Demonstrating compassion is often in conflict with getting things done in a busy world. Compassion for an individual in a class of many costs an unfair amount of time but the reward of exchanging your own self-worth for a moment of understanding another's problems is always greater than any loss involved."

Take a moment and reflect on the last time that you actually stopped to have that heart-to-heart conversation, and help your student Recognize their Teachable Moment without pressing forward? What did you sacrifice? What was the gift?

What trait is your greatest strength? When you take a look at all the character qualities listed, which one of those do you have that is really strong?

As I mentioned before, I have a double dose of enthusiasm and, although it can give me energy to move forward, without awareness I can sometimes be too enthusiastic. I may seem overbearing, hyperactive, or "control freaky." For me, one of the Teachable Moments regarding my character strength is balancing enthusiasm with some of my growth virtues, such as self-discipline, patience, discernment and trust. When I can leverage my strength virtue and balance it with a growth virtue, then I am at my most authentic and powerful self and can be of best use to myself and those around me.

Another teaching that really exemplifies Recognizing Teachable Moments for me is the essay "The Fence." "There was a little boy with a bad temper. His father gave him a bag of nails and told him that every time he lost his temper to hammer a nail in the back fence. The first day the boy had driven 37 nails into the fence. Then it gradually dwindled down.

He discovered it was easier to hold his temper than to drive those nails into the fence. Finally the day came when the boy did not lose his temper at all. He told his father about it and the father suggested that the boy now pull out one nail for each day that he was able to hold his temper. The days passed and the young boy was finally able to tell his father that all the nails were gone.

The father took his son by the hand and led him to the fence. He said, "You have done well my son, but look at the holes in the fence; the fence will never be the same. When you say things in anger they leave a scar just like this one. You can put a knife in a man and draw it out, it will not matter how many times you say I am sorry, the wound is still there. A verbal wound is as bad as a physical one."

With all humility I wish I knew who the author of this was. I Googled it and tried to find it but I couldn't. I send gratitude to this author for providing such a compelling illustration of the power of our words. This story serves as an excellent tool for strengthening detachment, discernment, self-discipline and empathy in helping us to guard our tongue so that we will not have to feel guilty, make amends and ask for forgiveness when we say things that we cannot take back.

In the original *Chicken Soup for the Soul* book by Jack Canfield and Mark Victor Hanson, there is a story called "All Good Things" shared by Sister Helen P. Mrosla. In the story she talks about how one day she asked her students to list the name of other students in the room on two sheets of paper, leaving a space between each name.

Then she told them to think of the nicest things they could say about each of their classmates and write it down. It took the remainder of the class period to finish the assignment and as the students left the room each one handed in their papers. That Saturday the teacher wrote down the name of each student on a separate piece of paper and listed what everyone else had said about that individual.

On Monday she gave each student his or her list. Before long the entire class was smiling. "Really?" she heard whispered. "I never knew that I meant anything to anyone and I didn't know others like me so much," were most of the comments. No one ever mentioned those papers in class again. She never knew if they discussed them after class or with their parents but it did not matter. The exercise had accomplished its purpose: the students were happy with themselves and one another. That group of students moved on.

Several years later one of the students was killed in Vietnam and the teacher attended the funeral of that special student. She had never seen a serviceman in a military coffin before; he looked so handsome, so mature. The church was packed with his friends. One-by-one those who loved him took a last walk by the coffin.

The teacher was the last one to bless the coffin. As she stood there one of the soldiers who acted as a pallbearer came up to her and asked, "Were you Mark's math teacher?" She nodded yes. Then he said, "Mark talked about you a lot."

After the funeral most of Mark's former classmates went together to a luncheon. Mark's mother and father were there waiting to speak with his teacher. "We want to show you something," his father said, taking a wallet out of his pocket. "They found this on Mark when he was killed; we thought you might recognize it."

Opening the billfold he carefully removed two worn pieces of notebook paper that had obviously been taped, folded and refolded many times. The teacher knew without looking that the papers were the ones on which she had listed all the good things each of Mark's classmates had said about him.

"Thank you so much for doing that," Mark's mother said. As you can see, Mark treasured it. All of Mark's former classmates started to gather around. Charlie smiled rather sheepishly and said, "I still have my list, it is in the top drawer of my desk at home. Chuck's wife said, "Chuck asked me to put his in our wedding album."

"I have mine too," Marilyn said, "it is in my diary." Then Vicky, another classmate, reached into her pocket book, took out her wallet and showed her worn and frazzled list to the group. "I carry this with me at all times," Vicky said, and without batting an eyelash she continued, "I think we all saved our lists."

That is when the teacher finally sat down and cried. She cried for Mark and for all his friends who would never see him again.

So in this Teachable Moment, it is a reminder for us to focus on what is good, acknowledge it and be a witness to it so that we can share that good with people around us, especially before it is too late. Research shows that it is important to be positive and say positive, encouraging things seven times more than negative. This is an activity that would be easy to do... not just with our students but with our staff members and perhaps even with our families.

Dignity

Dignity is a sense of worthiness and respect. It comes from remembering who we truly are and our purpose for being. When we are mindful of our own dignity, we hold ourselves with self-esteem, respect and simple confidence. We move and speak in a graceful manner. We avoid actions that cause us to feel ashamed. We recognize the inherent worth of each person, whether or not they see it for themselves. We treat everyone with the respect and honor all beings deserve. We refuse to violate anyone's rights. When we value each other, we honor our Creator.

The Virtues Project™

1 What is your strength virtue and how does it show up in your life?

2 What is your growth virtue? What steps can you take to strengthen it?

3 What lessons would be helpful for you to be learning at this time in your life?

Chapter Seven

Rules Broken, Promises Kept: The Art of Setting Clear Boundaries

"When the power of love overcomes the love of power, the world will know peace."

Jimmy Hendrix

Setting Clear Boundaries

The third strategy of The Virtues Project is Setting Clear Boundaries based on Restorative Justice. Boundaries based on respect and Restorative Justice create a climate of peace, cooperation and safety in our homes, schools and communities.

This strategy focuses on setting guidelines and ground rules that restore justice, engage cooperation and preserve courtesy. It calls for students to make amends, not excuses, and gives them reflection time rather than mere detention. It includes creating shared Class Promises or Classroom Constitutions to guide behavior throughout the school year. If students don't feel safe, they are not free to learn. If teachers don't feel safe, they are not free to teach.

The whole purpose of boundaries is about keeping us safe. During a Virtues Project workshop we use a story about young children on a playground to exemplify this point. Imagine young children playing on the playground near a busy road. The playground did not have a fence to keep them safe. As a result the young children stayed close together in the middle of the playground. But when the fence was built at the perimeter of the playground, the children scattered to all ends of the playground, because they knew where the boundaries were and that made them feel safe.

Kids and adults thrive when there are clear boundaries. They help keep us physically as well as emotionally safe. There is no second-guessing whether or not something is okay.

When I was teaching kindergarten the year that I was blessed with the Disney honor, we started off with the usual rules, stated in a positive manner:

Our Class Rules
1   We will keep our hands, feet and objects to ourselves.
2   We will raise our hand and wait to be called on.
3   One person will talk at a time.
4   We will walk carefully.
5   We will clean up when we are finished working.

After I learned about The Virtues Project, we changed our classroom rules to class promises, because we all know that rules are meant to be broken and promises are meant to be kept. Around January of that year, before we revised our rules, we took a look at what we had been doing with Coach John Wooden's Success Pyramid. We talked about the virtues we had been strengthening as well as our class rules and we replaced the rules with the following virtue statements:

Our Class Promises
1   We will be peaceful with our words and our actions.
2   We will be gentle with people and things.
3   We will be respectful of people and things.
4   We will be enthusiastic learners and always work with excellence.

Once we had Our Class Promises, any time my students had a mistaken behavior I could go back to them and say, "Are you working with excellence?" or "Remember, let's be gentle with people and things." Those principles and promises were our vision for the way that we wanted to be with one another in our classroom.

That same year my principal, Lee Derby, an amazing leader with incredible heart, gave the leadership team Diane Tracy's *Blue's Clues for Success – The Eight Secrets behind a Phenomenal Business* to read. At first glance we wondered, "Why are we reading this? We are not a business." Then we realized that we actually were in the business of educating students.

So what does *Blue's Clues* have to do with us as an educational organization? There were some incredible nuggets of insight in this book. For me the one that was most profound was "the secret of success." The secret of success was really about the mission statement that the producers had for their show. They did not realize that it would become their management philosophy as well.

The mission of the show is "to empower, challenge and build the self-esteem of preschoolers while making them laugh." Tracy writes, "It is precisely how they see their mission of leaders in terms of their staff. They work very hard at empowering their people, challenging them, building their self-esteem and providing a fun, enjoyable work environment. More than anything else it is their secret to their success."

The secret to success is focusing on living that mission and vision in all areas of our personal and professional lives.

Leading with Virtues

As we know, there are many forms of leadership. There can be the authoritative leader, the dictator and the democratic leader. The Virtues Project encourages leading from an educative model.

The Virtues Project Educator's Guide views different styles of leadership and authority on a continuum of effectiveness, from the least effective learning and character development to the most effective. The least effective style is permissive. It is when we are not focused and the boundaries are always changing. When the boundaries are always changing it creates a climate of chaos and confusion.

Another style of leadership is the dominant style. This leadership style is very controlling; the boundaries are exceedingly harsh and punitive. Often times this style is characterized by expressions like "because I said so" and "this is how it is going to be." The climate this creates is one of control and rebellion.

The "slider" is a leader who shifts back and forth between a place of control and loose boundaries. This climate can sometimes create a pleasant environment but other times it can be chaos and fear depending on the "slider's" mood.

The democratic model of leadership is focused on equality, and the boundaries are negotiable. There can be a mixture of unity and argumentativeness and, as a result, the process can take a lot of time. Everything is up for debate and discussion. The million dollar question – who is really the leader?—never gets answered.

When we come from the educative perspective, as in The Virtues Project, leadership is focused on virtues. The boundaries are educative and consistent; they are there for a reason. We let people know what those reasons are, what it looks like in terms of being enforced and what the positive and negative consequences are. The climate that this produces is one of peace and joy.

Take a moment to reflect on where you are in terms of your leadership style. For me, before learning about the educative model, not only was I a slider but I "ran all of the bases." I went from democratic to permissive to dominant. I was not consistent in the least. The educative model is much more in alignment with my values. What is at the heart of leadership is what is in the highest and greatest good for all, and for me those are the virtues.

The Loving Service of Authority

When we talk about authority in The Virtues Project, we are really talking about authority in terms of providing loving service. Not "because it is my way or the highway" or "because I said so." It is because we are coming from that place of confidence and strength. We are being true to the highest and greatest good for the learning, for the individual and for the organization.

We teach what we need to learn. I, who grew up in a boundary-less environment, am writing a chapter about setting clear boundaries, ha! The "boundaries" I grew up with were always changing; and I had no idea what healthy boundaries looked like.

Our family of origin helps to shape who we are and how we go about our work on a daily basis. When we are fully aware and understand that some things actually do come from our growing up and our childhood experiences, we open up to the learning process. And that is when we start to transform.

One of the activities that we do in a Virtues Project workshop goes like this (you may want to try this as you read along): We ask participants to take out a piece of paper and fold it into three equal rectangular sections. In the first section, draw a very small square, as teeny tiny as you can get. In the second section scribble from the top to the bottom, just scribble, scribble, scribble. In the third section, create an oval taking up as much space as you possibly can.

What do you think these three different drawings represent? They have to do with how you were raised in your family of origin. The small square represents a very controlling family. There are benefits and consequences as a result of growing up in a very controlling family. Adults who grew up in a very controlling family are often very controlling themselves, or have what Linda Kavelin-Popov refers to as "opposite-i-tis," which means going to the other extreme. They relinquish any kind of boundaries so their kids do not feel restricted the way they may have felt.

If you look at the second section it represents no boundaries; it is just chaos all over the place. For people who grew up in homes where there were no boundaries, oftentimes they created even stricter boundaries for themselves. They may have even punished themselves worse than anyone else could have punished them. They tried to make clarity out of that chaos. Because they did not have models for how to set clear boundaries as children, they often pass on the boundary-less society to their children. They often have a hard time being consistent and enforcing boundaries as adults.

The last section with that large oval is the educative model. This is a family where the boundaries are clear; there is space and freedom to live and grow; yet there is also that healthy circle of clear boundaries. There is no chaos and fear, but real clarity of what is expected.

Creating Healthy Boundaries

If we are not sure how to create healthy boundaries, here is a process that may help. First, think about a virtue. A good choice might be a virtue you want to bring into your classroom, your home, or your personal life.

Using the virtue "Orderliness" as an example, the ground rule in the classroom might be the following: Our classroom is a place of order; we put things back in their proper places. The ground rule is really the virtue of orderliness. The boundaries are those specific examples of what that looks like. Materials are put back in their proper places, desks are organized in a neat manner, personal belongings are hung up on the hooks in the closet, etc. These are the ground rules.

The last part of setting clear boundaries is focused on the consequences. If things are neat and orderly then the logical consequence is we have more time for learning or maybe have some extra free time because we are not spending so much time cleaning up. We know where things are and we can easily get them. If a student's desk is not orderly then one of the logical consequences might be that he or she comes in early or stays after school or during recess to make the desk neater.

If a student is not orderly and fails to turn in his homework, the logical consequence is that it will not get marked and that student will get a zero or a late grade for turning it in late. If a student borrows something and he forgets to put it back then perhaps he will not have the opportunity to borrow that in the future and will have to bring in his own materials.

Class Meetings

One of the ways to come up with these ground rules with your students is to have class meetings. Class meetings are a great tool for strengthening your class community. There are many resources out there that can help you set up a class meeting.

Ideally you want to arrange the group in a circle so everyone can have eye contact and everybody is on the same level playing field. It is often good to sit on the floor and choose two student leaders.

Donna Styles, author of *Class Meetings – Building Leadership, Problem Solving and Decision Making Skills in the Respectful Classroom*, outlines things that teachers as well as students can do during class meetings. She says teachers should act as coaches providing guidance to the leader whenever necessary. They can also fulfill the role as the group secretary. She suggests that teachers can also be part of the membership of the group. By offering information only when needed and making comments only when necessary, we can help keep the tone positive and helpful.

She goes on to explain the student leaders' roles. It is their job to keep the meeting running smoothly, open and close the meeting, follow an orderly process for conducting the meeting, and follow steps for solving problems. They need to model their leadership by becoming active participants and making eye contact with each person speaking. It is their job to keep the discussion on topic and to guide students back to order if they go off topic. Also, the student leaders will want to ask questions and clarify or restate any problems or ideas that come up. Finally, they have the responsibility of summarizing what was said.

When an issue arises in the classroom or when the teacher wants some information and is coming from that educative perspective, either the teacher or students can call a class meeting. The kids get into a circle and the question or the problem is presented. The student leaders help to facilitate problem solving and brainstorming in order to build consensus about what to do next.

It can be a small issue like, what is the best way for us to line up in an orderly manner? Or it can be more serious such as, we have a student who is being bullied and left out, how can we best handle the situation?

The Responsive Classroom approach includes a morning meeting, which is focused more on community building and less on problem solving. The purpose of a morning meeting is fivefold. First, a morning meeting sets the tone for respectful learning and establishes a climate of trust. Second, the tone and climate of the morning meeting extends beyond the meeting. Third, a morning meeting motivates children by addressing two human needs: the need to feel a sense of significance and belonging, and the need to have fun. The fourth purpose is that many ordinary moments of respectful interaction in morning meetings produce some extraordinary moments. Finally, morning meetings merge social, emotional and intellectual learning.

Many schools are using PBIS (Positive Behavioral Interventions and Supports). They create clear and consistent expectations, usually focused on respect, responsibility and readiness to learn. What does respect look like in the classroom, in the hallway, the bathroom and the cafeteria? What do responsibility and readiness to learn look like in all of these areas?

In CEP's *Eleven Principles Sourcebook, Guidebook 7 on Intrinsic Motivation*, Dr. Merle Schwartz, past Director of Education and Research for CEP, offers us the following way to view the connection between PBIS and character education: "In 1997, the Individuals with Disabilities Education Act (IDEA) was amended to include positive behavioral interventions and supports (PBIS) as the recommended method for dealing with challenging behavior in children with disabilities. PBIS is an approach that assists students in learning prosocial behavior through, modeling, shaping, cueing, and dialoguing in an environment that is respectful of individual student needs. The PBIS process provides a better understanding of why challenging behavior occurs, i.e., what function the behavior serves, when it happens, what influences it, and what maintains it. In contrast, behavior management systems seek to control student behavior through external inducements that do not teach deficit skills nor develop greater self-awareness in students.

PBIS and character education are natural partners for improving the educational experience of children with significant behavioral and learning challenges.

Both honor the students' learning needs by developing student autonomy, a sense of belonging, and competence. Throughout the PBIS process, teachers utilize the strategies of reflection, problem solving, restitution, and social skill training, as appropriate and based on the cognitive ability of the student.

In PBIS, extrinsic rewards and consequences are at times necessary to reduce the problem behavior while the student is learning the replacement social skills. For example, a teacher might help a student track their success in keeping their relationships with others nonaggressive by having the student record a tally for each designated period of time they are prosocial in meeting their needs. A certain number of tallies may be traded for special time playing a game with a classmate. While the child is "earning" special time, they are also learning prosocial behavior. From a character education perspective, individual plans should be monitored closely so that as students begin to gain control of their emotions and find more appropriate means for communication, reinforcement moves away from extrinsic rewards and towards social rewards, ultimately emphasizing students' intrinsic satisfaction in being a good citizen of the school and classroom. This is a much easier process in schools that fosters character development within a caring atmosphere."

Focusing solely on giving out coupons is in direct opposition to the latest research on intrinsic motivation, specifically addressed in Daniel Pink's book *Drive*. Giving out coupons also runs counter to Carol Dweck's work regarding mindsets. Imagine students who have been continuously put down, labeled or punished. Those students may feel like they have no chance of earning any of the coupons because they feel they are "bad."

They do not see their own gifts of character in themselves and do not believe that they have "good" in them.

If you are a school that uses the PBIS coupon system, I encourage you to consider also verbally acknowledging the student, spelling out exactly how the student displayed the positive behavior and the virtue they exemplified. Then the interaction becomes more than just something they can turn in for a reward; it helps to strengthen their intrinsic motivation and helps them realize they have that virtue in them. It is important to be extremely mindful of witnessing the virtues in the students whose behaviors are often challenging. By honoring the virtues you witness in them, you help them to develop those virtues and strengthen their authentic self-esteem.

The Process of Restorative Justice

What happens when there is a mistaken behavior? Are students sent down to the office when there is a fight? Are they put into time out or even worse, suspended? Do they have the opportunity to reflect or make amends? When we use the process of Restorative Justice it helps students understand what happened and take responsibility for what they did.

In the ideal process of Restorative Justice, students:
- Take responsibility for what they do in order to...
- Make restitution, which results in...
- Reconciliation, which is to make friends again, which...
- Restore the relationship and restore the offender to the community.

Forgiveness alone is not enough. Justice requires there be some amends, an action or gesture to fix the problem, with the offender taking responsibility instead of merely being punished. In the ideal situation, there is also reconciliation, restoring friendship and contentment on all sides with the outcomes.

The Four Steps to Restore Justice

1 Ask all involved what happened. Use "how" and "what "questions, not "why".
2 Ask what virtue was missing to create the conflict.
3 Ask what it would look like if they had used the missing virtue.
4 Ask how they can make an amends.

When someone makes amends, it is not about just making the person who was harmed feel better. It is also about the person who made the mistake. That person needs to realize he made a mistake, not that he is a mistake.

So what does Restorative Justice look like in action? The first time I experienced Restorative Justice my kids were at home alone on a Monday night. My daughter is a dancer and my son is a football player. If you know anything about Monday night television, at least in our house, it is "Dancing with the Stars" and "Monday Night Football." My husband and I were out at an event when I got the phone call.

"Mom, Jake will not let me watch 'Dancing with the Stars'," my daughter cried. Then Jake got on the phone, "Dani will not let me watch 'Monday Night Football'." After hearing both sides of the issue, I guided my kids back to the family ground rules we had set when we chose our family's core virtues. I asked them if they knew what the consequence was if they could not be respectful of one another. They told me the consequence was they needed to go to their rooms to figure out a way they could be respectful towards one another and resolve this in a peaceful way. They knew what to do, and I hoped they followed through.

The next day we were sitting at breakfast and I went through the Restorative Justice process with them. I asked both of them to tell me what had happened. They both shared their side of the story.

I asked them to tell me what virtue was missing. It was two hours worth of TV and they both wanted to watch something different. They decided the virtue that would be most helpful was flexibility. I said okay, and asked them to describe how they would use flexibility in the future and what it would look like.

They agreed that my daughter could watch "Dancing with the Stars" the first hour and then my son could watch "Monday Night Football" during the second hour because it is the end of the football game that is most important.

The last step was to make an amends, so I asked them how they could make amends to one another. They both apologized, gave each other a hug, and then they made the commitment to be more flexible and honor the wishes of one another in the future.

When they got up to leave the table they gave me this weird look and my daughter said, "Wow Mom, this stuff really works!" Sibling rivalry ended that day in my home; my kids now have a strategy they can use to work through things on their own.

Many schools already have peer mediators or peacemakers. We can add to the peacemaking skills by teaching them the process of Restorative Justice and allowing them to help facilitate individuals going through this process. We can also teach students to go through this process by themselves.

Peace Zone

One of the ways to help kids resolve conflict is to create a "peace zone" whether at home or in school. A peace zone is an area in the classroom, cafeteria or another place where students can go to calm down and/or reflect. You may wish to have materials such as puppets, playdough, stuffed animals, journals, markers or a stress ball in this zone. Sometimes it is helpful when students have the opportunity to use their hands to work out their anger and frustrations in a peaceful way.

You may want to invite your children to help create and decorate the peace zone. In addition, it is helpful to model how and when to use the peace zone to solve problems. It is also helpful to have a peace zone poster on the wall for students to follow:

Steps to Creating Peace

1 Take turns truthfully telling your experience of what happened.
2 Listen respectfully to the other person's point of view.
3 Share how you honestly felt.

4   Creatively find a virtue you each need.
5   Use justice and forgiveness to decide what amends need to be made.
6   Practice commitment to decide how to do it differently next time. Congratulations, you have solved your problem peacefully.

Can you imagine if we all went through this process, not just taught it to our students, but used it in our own lives as well?

In *The Power of Guidance – Teaching Social/Emotional Skills in Early Childhood Classroom* by Dan Gartrell, he writes about how misbehavior makes us think of punishing. Mistaken behavior makes us think of guiding and educating.

There is a graphic report done in cartoon illustrations from "The Advancement Project." Sadly it is called "The School to Prison Pipeline Report." In this report are statistics and voices from youth saying how zero tolerance just does not work. It talks about how many of our kids who get into trouble really need some guidance.

They need adults and educators to witness the good, to acknowledge their strengths and to guide them when they have mistaken behaviors through the Restorative Justice Process. We need to do this so that these young people can learn and develop their virtues. They are desperate for alternative solutions to their mistaken behaviors. Unfortunately, oftentimes no one has taken the time to teach these kids what to do and how to act properly so they end up getting into trouble because that is all they know.

I am grateful that the Advancement Project's "Telling It Like It Is: Youth Speak Out On The School to Prison Pipeline" report advocates for the Restorative Justice Process. It is a significant paradigm shift away from the punitive discipline that happens in most schools.

Finally, when we think about Setting Clear Boundaries, it is important to be moderate and have no more than four or five stated boundaries. We want them to be specific to show the exact behavior and what it looks like in action. We want to frame it in the positive, what we *will* do, not what we will not do.

We want to give specific, relevant and meaningful consequences for bottom line behaviors. We want to use consequences that are not punitive but are educative. It is important that we are consistent and follow through; it is also important that we communicate these rules clearly.

We need to be sure that students understand the virtues that are involved. When they are on the receiving end of consequences, they need to know that it is about learning and growing, not about punishment. The bottom line rules are non-negotiable, and promises and commitments are non-negotiable. Finally, we need to be assertive in making our expectations clear, not being wishywashy but standing firm.

Coming from a place of authority and loving service helps people to feel safe. When people are clear about the boundaries they are able to grow to their fullest capacity as a result.

Justice

Justice is being fair in all that we do. We continually look for the truth, not bowing to others' judgments or perceptions. We do not backbite. We clear up problems face to face. We make agreements that benefit everyone equally. When we commit a wrong, we are honest in correcting it and making amends. If someone is hurting us, it is just to stop them. It is never just for strong people to hurt weaker people. With justice, we protect everyone's rights. Sometimes when we stand for justice, we stand alone.

The Virtues Project™

1 What is your leadership style and how is it working for you? Are you more proactive or reactive?
2 How comfortable are you with setting and reinforcing boundaries? If you are not very comfortable, what would help you become more comfortable and confident?
3 Describe your classroom management. Are your expectations clear and your consequences logical, consistent and educative?

Chapter Eight

Honoring the Nobility in Us All

*"More important than being successful is being significant.
Significance means making a contribution to others."*
Stephen Covey

The definition of spirituality in The Virtues Project is "that which gives meaning and purpose to one's life." When I first started speaking around the world doing workshops for educators about "The Five Strategies of The Virtues Project," I found that if the word "virtues" did not cause educators to put up some resistance, then the word "spirituality" often did.

People would think the project was religious, aligned with a certain political party or some kind of New Age fad. They did not realize that meaning and purpose are what drive us all. The reason we became educators, or doctors, or nurses or parents is to fulfill the human longing for meaning and purpose. That is the foundation for our definition of spirituality.

In Daniel Pink's book *A Whole New Mind – Why the Right Brainer Will Rule the Future*, he devotes an entire chapter to "Meaning." He writes, "As well-known molecular biologist Eric Lander told the crowd, science is merely one way to understand the world. Across many different realms there is growing recognition that spirituality, not religion necessarily, but the more broadly defined concern for the meaning and purpose of life is a fundamental part of the human condition. Indeed our capacity for faith again, not religion per se, but the belief in something larger than ourselves may be wired into our brains. Perhaps not surprisingly this wiring seems to run through the brain's right hemisphere."

Mr. Pink goes on to talk about another field that has begun to take spirituality more seriously: business. He writes, "If the conceptual age is flowering with post-materialistic values and deepening our 'meaning want', it makes sense that the phenomenon would take root in the place where many of us spend most of our waking hours."

He continues, "Most of the executives define spirituality in much the same way. Not as religion but as a basic desire to find purpose and meaning in one's life. He also goes on to say "yet the executives were so understandably concerned that the language of spirit in the workplace would offend their religiously diverse employees that they scrubbed their vocabulary of all of such talk."

We see this in education as well. When we talk about virtues or values, people get scared. Those old enough to remember think back to the 1970's when there was the Values Clarification Movement. Many people felt that schools became too "touchy feely," and were more concerned with developing students' self-esteem than really developing the whole child and their capabilities.

If that wasn't scary enough, people were also concerned with *whose* values we were teaching. Now we have come to a common understanding that virtues are universal positive qualities of character; they really are at the heart of what meaning and purpose is all about.

We are starting to see in the news and hear all over that people are "parched," thirsty for this meaning and purpose in their lives. Parker Palmer, author of *The Courage to Teach* as well as several other inspiring books, refers to it as a "hidden wholeness, the journey toward an undivided life." When we bring our whole being to the work we do, we actually are more capable and productive. The bottom line increases as a result of our joy and satisfaction increasing.

In the late Rachel Kessler's book *The Soul of Education – Helping Students Find Connection, Compassion and Character in School,* she writes of the "seven gateways to the soul" in education. She describes a yearning for deep connection, a longing for silence and solitude, the search for meaning and purpose, the hunger for joy and delight, the creative drive, the urge for transcendence and the need for initiation.

Young people's strength virtue is idealism. We need to give them a positive way to make their mark on the world or run the risk that they will make their mark in a negative way.

As Parker Palmer wrote in the forward of *The Soul of Education*, "Without healthy forms led by responsible adults, young people will seek these gateways on their own, sometimes in destructive ways like drugs, sex, suicide, hazing and even murder. Helping students find constructive ways to express their longings increases their motivation to learn, stay in school, strengthens ties to family and friends, and approach adult life with vitality, character and vision."

This is very similar to Bob Solo's philosophy in his book *Activating the Desire to Learn* in which he expounds upon William Glasser's (1998) choice theory. Solo explains, "Motivation goes beyond just physical needs for survival, but we actually have four basic psychological needs that must be satisfied to be emotionally healthy. These strongly apply to school and learning:

- We need belonging or connecting. The need for belonging or connecting motivates us to develop relationships and cooperate with others. Building a spirit of connection and community is essential to creating a need-satisfying school characterized by high achievement.
- We need power or competence; we need to be able to feel empowered that we are capable of doing something. Power is achieved through competence, achievement and mastery. One of our jobs as educators is to teach kids how to be powerful in a responsible way.
- We need freedom; freedom of choice, giving students voice and choice over not necessarily what they will learn but that how they can go about learning it. As humans we are motivated to be free, to choose. Effective teachers help students follow the drive to be free in a way that is respectful to others. Students who are given free-

dom within safe and clear boundaries are free to thrive, while students who perceive themselves as not having a voice or choice will oftentimes behave in ways that are disruptive, interfere with learning and can be physically and emotionally harmful to themselves and others.

- We need some fun: A joyless classroom never inspires students to do high quality academic work on a regular basis. When teachers and kids are having fun, learning is deeper and stronger, and students maintain the keen desire to learn that characterizes early childhood learning centers."

When we are having fun, learning is deeper and stronger. Here is an exercise you may wish to try with your class next time they could use a little "brain break" or energy boost. Invite your students to think about what brings them joy. Play some joyful music and ask students to walk around the room until the music stops. When the music stops, have them turn to someone standing next to them and tell their partner something that brings them joy. Turn the music back on, have the students continue to walk around the room. When you stop the music again, have them tell something else that brings them joy to another person standing near them. Do this a few times, and then have the kids sit down. Notice the energy, the smiles on their faces and then the purposefulness and productivity that happen as a result.

Another activity that you can do is to ask students to bring in an object that symbolizes something that is important in their life right now. Have them put it in a paper bag. You can do this as a staff developer as well.

Rachel Kessler describes this activity in her book. "When the students have brought their objects and they leave the room, the teacher takes the items out of the bags and puts them on the table. Each student is asked to come up one at a time, choose an item and see if they can identify who brought in that item.

"Once they have identified the person who brought the item in they ask the question, 'What does this mean to you, what is the story?' The student gets to tell the significance of why they brought their item in." It is a way to really connect kids and open them up on a deeper level so that the intimacy they share is even greater. (A definition of intimacy I learned in Al-Anon that I feel is really profound is "in to me you see.")

Paper bag stories help to strengthen community and build empathy. Because each story comes straight from the heart, the kids are more engaged and open to listening. It is imperative that we give our kids and ourselves many opportunities for authentic engagement and time for everyone to share their stories.

The Power of Affirmations

One of my dear friends, probably the most creative poet I have ever known, is Barbara Tally. In her book *Tally Up – The Excitement of Value Based Living* she teaches us how to create affirmations. I encourage you to create your own affirmations and work with your students using this process. Here are the steps Barbara suggests:

- "After careful reflection time decide what is most important to you. You may be able to do anything but you still cannot do everything. And there are some things you can do that you should not do. Make sure that the affirmation is in alignment with your vision and values.
- Visualize in your mind today what the achievement will look or feel like. Make your goals clear, the clearer the picture the better the result. Everything that you want is first created in your mind.
- State succinctly what you have already created and affirmed in your mind. Write down the affirmations making sure they are clear, short, in the present tense, positive and from a spiritual perspective, that meaning and purpose place.
- Write your affirmations on index cards and place them in locations where you will be reminded of them often.
- Focus energy on your goal or vision consistently. The more energy you give to an idea the quicker you will realize it. Your visions can become reality with faith, focus, energy and action.

- Believe and have faith in your affirmation and recite it at every opportunity. Celebrate your affirmation and feel the feeling as if you have already realized it."

This is echoed in the writings of Jack Canfield's book, *The Success Principles: How To Get From Where You Are To Where You Want To Be* and is confirmed in the actions of many Olympic Gold Medalists. They go through this process and say their affirmations; they really visualize all of their dreams coming true. They go through each step in their mind's eye and when they are hooked up to electrodes their brain waves show that the brain does not know the difference between whether you really have manifested your goal or you are just acting it out.

This is a great way to create the brain waves and patterns that really spur you on to success. I encourage you to create your own affirmations and work with your students to create theirs. It is great to have personal affirmations, class affirmations and school affirmations; let it become that which goes into your mind automatically and changes the negative tape to something positive.

For example, *I am happy, peaceful and relaxed. I successfully empower my students to thrive each day. I work with excellence, ease and grace.*

Honoring the spirit is all about joy, meaning and purpose. It could be the arts, service learning, service leadership, nature, traditions, celebrations, prayer or meditation. It can be whatever honors your own spirit and that of the group's.

Jim Wood's book *Yardsticks – Children in the Classroom Ages 4 to 14, a Resource for Parents and Teachers*, is actually a great tool for honoring the spirit. It gets to the developmentally appropriate continuum of students and helps us as educators meet students where they are. In his book Wood goes over the different domains of a child and their growth patterns: the physical domain, the social domain, the language and the cognitive. He talks about vision and fine and gross motor ability.

At the beginning of his book, *Childhood, and a Multi-Cultural View*, Melvin Konner includes a great quote. He says, "In order to be treated fairly and equally children have to be treated differently." How do you differentiate in your classroom? Is it just by skill and ability, or do you do it by your students' interests, passion and what brings them joy, meaning and purpose?

What honors your spirit, what honors the individual spirits of the people in your classroom, in your school community and beyond? How often do you really take time to listen to your spirit?

Do you have a favorite song or do you like to go for a walk out in nature? Is there a particular cup of tea that you enjoy drinking while talking with a friend? It is important for us as educators to honor our own spirit, to put our oxygen masks on first so we can be of service to our students and practice and model self-care.

In Clifton Taulbert's book *Eight Habits of the Heart for Educators – Making Strong School Communities through Timeless Values,* he suggests an activity to do with our students to build unselfishness in our school. First, have students define their ideal school community. Ask them to list what they need from their peers to create their ideal. Then pick the top five or ten unselfish actions and make them into a poster they can display and refer to during the school year. This helps to build a caring community. When we make those virtues visible they become a tangible reminder to automatically honor our spirit and help us to live our highest selves every day.

Another great way to honor the spirit is to focus on gratitude by writing what we are grateful for every day -- a gratitude list. When we are grateful and appreciative toward others, it not only makes the other person feel better, but it raises our own vibration as well.

The book *Every Monday Matters – 52 Ways to Make a Difference* by Matthew Emerzin and Kelly Bozza offers an interesting suggestion on the 29th Monday: write a note of gratitude. In their book they show an uncanny picture of the statistics illustrating how many emails, text messages and pieces of junk mail we get, and how very few personal letters we receive. It is helpful to think about a person who we have not spoken to in a long time that we may want to thank for what they have brought to our life.

They suggest a postcard, a letter or other card and take a few minutes to write a warm and sincere message that clearly communicates your love and appreciation for that person. You can decide if you want to add any special touches like unique paper or scents or photographs, drawings on the envelope or a special stamp. Once you write that letter of gratitude, send it and see what happens! This book includes 51 more ways to honor the spirit and make every Monday matter.

Service learning, which is different from community service, is another way to honor the spirit. According to the National Service Learning Clearance House, "Service learning is a teaching and learning strategy that integrates meaningful community service with instruction and reflection to enrich the learning experience, teach civic responsibility and strengthen communities."

Authentic service learning experiences, while almost endlessly diverse, have some common characteristics (Eyler and Giles *Where's the Learning in Service Learning*, 1999):

- They are positive, meaningful and real to participants.
- They involve cooperative rather than competitive experiences and thus promote skills associated with teamwork and community involvement and citizenship.
- They address complex problems in complex settings rather than simplified problems in isolation.
- They offer opportunities to engage in problem solving by requiring participants to gain knowledge of the specific context of their service learning activity and community challenges rather than only to draw a picture in our lives or abstract knowledge such as might come from a textbook. As a result service learning offers powerful opportunities to acquire the habits of critical thinking, i.e.: the ability to identify the most important questions or issues within a real world situation.
- They promote deeper learning because results are immediate and uncontrived. There are no right answers in the back of the book.
- As a consequence of immediacy of experience service learning is more likely to be personally meaningful to participants and to generate emotional consequences to

challenge values as well as ideas and hence to support social, emotional and cognitive learning and development.

In addition to service learning for authentic learning, what
does all of this honoring the spirit have to do with our work
as educators? As Eric Jensen described in his book *Brain Based
Learning*, "We learn best with our minds, hearts and bodies engaged. The more aspects of self we can tap into for learners the
more effective we will be as educators."

He goes on to say that, "What this means to us as educators
is that the emotional state of your learners is at least as important as the intellectual, cognitive content of your presentation.
Never void emotions, deal with them gently and personally.
Allow negative ones to be processed and positive ones to be
celebrated.

Enlist positive emotional states from learners with enjoyable
activities, games, humor, personal attention and acts of caring.
Reflect on your priorities as a teacher, do you put your learners
emotions and feelings on par with mastery of content and skill
learning, remember the two are directly biologically linked."

He offers three immediate strategies for providing alternative productive outlets for what are basically powerful, biolog-
ical expressions:

- We establish new positive and productive rituals such
  as arrival handshakes, music, fanfare, positive greetings,
  hugs, high fives, etc.
- Set a tone of teamwork with class rituals such as team
  names, cheers, gestures, games and friendly competition.
- Encourage participation rituals such as class applause
  when learners contribute or present, closing rituals with
  songs, affirmations, discussions, journal writing, cheers,
  self-assessment gestures, etc. Add your own personal
  form of ritual to celebrate a learner's achievement such
  as a special student award, virtues acknowledgement
  sent home, extra privileges, etc.

There are countless ways to honor the spirit of your students, the classroom, your school as a whole and your own personal spirit. Whenever you have assemblies or pep rallies, go to football games or other school activities, you honor the spirit of the community. Your cheers, your chants, your fight songs, the colors that you wear all honor the spirit.

Cari Matejka, an amazing teacher in the small town of Olean, New York, honors the spirit of her fifth grade students by helping them publish the *World Changer Exclusive*. It is a monthly publication in which students take a closer look at virtues. They have featured items such as the virtues they are "growing" each month. They interview leaders and others in their local community and write about the virtues that they see. They give virtues acknowledgements to their teachers and to their parents. They reflect on their Teachable Moments and how specific virtues have helped them to strengthen their own character. They even write advertisements and "Wanted" posters for specific virtues. They incorporate digital pictures, photos, word searches and games into their newspaper as well as original poems and other types of writing. This publication comes out regularly and is deeply inspiring.

One of the second grade teachers I had the honor of working with when I was an instructional coach in DC Public Schools has a way to honor the spirit of her students after she reads Todd Parr's book *It's OK To Be Different* to her class. She has her students create their own "*It's OK*" book. In this book, beautifully illustrated by second graders, they write, "It's OK to be short," "It's OK to be tackled in football," "It's OK to have a Koosh ball," "It's OK to have a birthmark," "It's OK to cry," "It's OK to have a short mom," "It's OK to have light skin," "It's OK not to have sisters," and so on. They know that it is OK to be different, and that uniqueness is what makes each of us special.

"Mama Kay" and "Mama Rashida" of Wombwork Productions are two more women whom I have had the privilege to watch honor the spirit in powerful ways. They go into communities, prisons, and schools, working with people to transform challenges into gifts. They do it through movement, songs, chants, tribal dance and music, and they create powerful, moving, transformative experiences. I encourage you to check out the inspiring videos on their website at www.wombwork.com.

While enjoying the pleasure of doing virtues workshops in the Virgin Islands, I had the opportunity to work with a wonderfully committed educator, Sue Diverio, who works with people who had dropped out of school. She gave them hope by helping them write their stories and identifying a virtue they wanted to strengthen. She taught them how their virtues are the next step to moving them forward in their lives.

Sue was trained as a Freedom Writer's teacher under Erin Gruwell. Not only did Sue work with folks in St. Croix, she also brought some of her young angels, a group of high school youth she works with, to a school in New Jersey. There these incredible young people spent a week working with pre-K through 8th grade students at Resurrection School, facilitating virtues related activities and helping the students create their own virtues book. Resurrection is a Peaceable School and lives the virtues in such meaningful ways on a daily basis. Their book included something from every student, whether it was a story, poem, illustration or photo and each entry described how they saw the virtues exemplified in one another.

With access to the Internet and the ease of creating videos, now students have the opportunity to get their messages out globally. iEARN, the International Education and Resource Network, is an online community committed to making the world a better place. All of their projects have technology and global connections and they use both of those to provide opportunities for students to make a difference in the world.

Some of the programs that they have include the Bully Project, the Teddy Bear Project and more. When students have the opportunity to work on a global scale it helps them develop empathy and appreciation for one another.

One other project I am involved with is the My Hero Project. This project uses the power of media and technology to inspire, educate and empower people around the world. The project presents stories, art and short films that illuminate heroes from all walks of life, and across religious, cultural and political boundaries to build a global learning community.

The Virtues Project has partnered with the My Hero Project to create a Heroic Virtues Forum (www.myhero.com/go/forum). The My Hero website honors heroes of all ages from all walks of life. They are celebrated for the content of their character as much as the actions they have undertaken. It is through their strength of character and generosity of courage that they inspire others.

The Heroic Virtues Forum asks participants to share their insights on what qualities make someone a hero. Through discussion boards and various threads, visitors can read essays and posts, and contribute their own ideas about the following characteristics of heroes: vision, humility, love, faith, perseverance, joy, honesty or hope.

Or they can do a virtues pick and view a card on a specific trait to generate reflection and discussion. There are also lesson plans for educators to provide more structured activities on the anatomy of a heroic action.

One of our local heroes, whom I have written about in this book, is Mattie Stepaneck. He is part of the My Hero Project for his virtue of strength.

What are some ways that you can honor your own spirit? My website *www.virtuesproject.org* offers a variety of tools you can use. On the right hand side you can "click" and do a Virtues Pick. Doing a Virtues Pick can help whenever you want more clarity or insight for a situation or issue. When you read the card think about how it resonates with you. You can also share this with another person.

Dr. Dan Popov created an issue oriented "Five Card Spread" as another way to help you honor your spirit and gain clarity around a specific issue. A "Five Card Spread" is similar to a Virtues Pick. Simply focus on a question or an issue in your life. Then randomly select five virtues cards. (If you have a set of Virtues Reflection Cards you may wish to use them. If not, you can go to my website to do a spread online. First, go to the "Personal" section of the website and click on "Five Card Spread." Once there, click the Virtues links to build your Five Card Spread. After selecting all five links, move your mouse over your selections at the bottom to review the virtues you've selected.)

Each virtue has a specific relevance:

1 CORE VIRTUE - Identify the core virtue that applies in this situation, one that is at the heart of the matter.
2 GUIDING VIRTUE – Pick the virtue that will guide you and set your direction.
3 STRENGTH VIRTUE – This is the virtue you can rely on to keep you strong and purposeful.
4 CHALLENGE VIRTUE – This is the Growth Virtue you will need to cultivate in order to succeed. You need to remain mindful to practice this virtue.
5 SUSTAINING VIRTUE – This is the virtue that will support you to go the distance as you resolve this issue.

Try to hold these virtues in mind for at least a week after doing the Five Card Spread. Practice them mindfully and journal the results. The clarity and peace of mind you will find will be amazing

One of my favorite ways of honoring the spirit is by listening to music. I have playlists that get me "pumped," make me feel peaceful, and inspire me to action. Some of the songs on my playlist that inspire me are:

"Fantasy" by Earth, Wind and Fire
"Greatest Love of All" by Whitney Houston
"I Hope You Dance" by Leanne Rimes
"I'm Not Lost I am Exploring" by Jana Stanfield
"My Wish" by Rascal Flatts
"Seasons of Love" from Rent
"Strangely Wrapped Gift" by Red Grammer
"The Power of the Dream" by Celine Dion
"Walking on Sunshine" by Katrina and the Waves

If music is something that inspires you as well, I encourage you to create your own motivational playlists. Invite your students and colleagues to share their favorite songs and create a school wide motivational playlist. Give a "shout out" each day to a student, class or colleague and share their favorite song as part of the morning announcements. You will be surprised to see and hear how this practice helps to strengthen the connections be-tween people in your school.

Another activity is a "Virtues Healing Circle" or a "Virtues Sharing Circle." I had the honor of working with the founders of The Virtues Project at a high school in a rural town in Idaho where a young woman who was a junior in high school had been murdered. She was stabbed 29 times to death by two boys who were her friends. Overwhelming pain and hurt filled that community as a result. Imagine the fear you would feel if one of your friends was murdered by another friend. Who do you trust?

We were invited to do a workshop with educators and to do some family outreach followed by a healing circle with the youth. There was a circle of about 20 students. Our boundaries were for us to let them know we knew they had been through a really hard time and that there were some things that would be helpful to let go of in order to move forward.

The parameter of the sharing circle was for each person to share what was on his/her mind and heart, pick a virtues card randomly, read both sides out loud and then share if there was any wisdom or insight that he/she gleaned from reading that card. Then two of the participants in the circle would give an acknowledgment.

We went around the circle and people could pass, but then were given the opportunity to share again at the end. It took about 90 minutes and lots of tears, but at the end of the time the kids got up and hugged one another. There was forgiveness, understanding and relief. As a result, they made the commit-ment to bring The Virtues Project into not just their high school community but the community beyond.

The "Virtues Sharing Circle" is a very powerful way to help someone to share what is on his/her mind and heart and to be witnessed, held and understood. It provides the opportunity for significant healing to take place. Boundaries are clear and there is no cross talk; you share what is on your mind and heart, pick a card, share how that card resonates with you and then people give acknowledgements and you go to the next person.

As I am sure you have gathered from this chapter, the number of ways to honor ones' spirit is limitless. It is really about getting to know the individual students and yourself that provides the clarity about which way works best when Honoring the Spirit.

I would like to conclude this chapter with a story called "Animal School" by R.Z. Greenwald. It is about honoring individual learning styles and strengths in our children.

Animal School
Transcribed (and slightly modified) from:
Preparing Our Children for Success by R.Z. Greenwald

Once upon a time the animals had a school. They had to create a curriculum that would satisfy everyone, so they chose four subjects... running, climbing, flying and swimming. All the animals, of course, studied all the subjects.

The duck was very good at swimming, better than the teacher, in fact. He received passing grades in running and flying, but was hopeless in climbing, So they made him drop swimming so that he could practice climbing. After a while he was only average at swimming, but average is still acceptable, at least in school, and nobody worried much about it except the duck.

The eagle was considered a troublemaker. In his climbing class he beat everybody to the top of the tree, but he had his own way of getting there that was against the rules. He always had to stay after school and write, "cheating is wrong" five hundred times. That kept him from soaring, which he loved, but schoolwork comes first.

The bear flunked because they said he was lazy, especially in winter. His best time was summer, but school wasn't open then.

The zebra played hooky a lot because the ponies made fun of his stripes, and this made him very sad.

The kangaroo started out at the top of the racing class but became discouraged when he was told to move swiftly on all four legs the way his classmates did.

The fish quit school because he was bored. To him, all four subjects were the same, but nobody understood that because they had never seen a fish before.

The squirrel got an A in climbing but his flying teacher made him start from the ground up, instead of from the treetop down. His legs got sore from practicing takeoffs so that he began getting Cs in climbing and Ds in running.

The bee was the biggest problem of all so the teacher sent him to Doctor Owl for testing. Doctor Owl said that the bee's wings were too small for flying and they were in the wrong place. The bee never saw Doctor Owl's report so he just went ahead and flew anyway. I think I know a bee or two, how about you? The duck is the child who does well in math and poorly in English and is given tutorials by the English teacher while his classmates are doing math. He loses his edge in math, and only does passably well in English.

The eagle is the child who is turned into a troublemaker because he has his "own style" of doing things. While he is not doing anything "wrong," his non-conforming is perceived as troublesome for which he is punished.

Who does not recognize the bear? The kid who is great in camp, thrives on extra-curricular, but really just goes flat in the academics.

The zebra is the heavy, tall, short, or self-conscious kid whose failure in school few realize is due to a sense of social inadequacy.

The kangaroo is the one who instead of persevering gives up and becomes that discouraged child whose future disappears because he was not appreciated.

The fish is the child who really requires full special education and should not be in the regular classroom.

The squirrel, unlike the duck who "manages," becomes a failure.

The bee, oh the bee, is the child who the school feels it cannot deal with, yet against all odds, with the backing of his parents, has enough self-motivation to do well even though everyone thought he couldn't. I had the pleasure of knowing many bees.

Each child is a unique blend of talents, personality and ingredients.

Some children are skilled intellectually, others are blessed emotionally, and many more are born with creative ingenuity. Each child possesses his/her very exclusive collection of gifts.

Your students did not come with a direction book. Effective teachers are always learning, studying and customizing the instructions for their individual students. Each and every child is as unique as their fingerprints, a sparkling diamond of unparalleled beauty.

Don't let your students become a kangaroo!

"Animal School" Reflection Questions

1   Could you identify with any of the animals, personally or as a parent/teacher?
2   Why did the animals take the same subjects?
3   Did the animals benefit from taking the same subjects? Explain your answer.
4   Why do you think the squirrel wasn't allowed to fly down from the top of the tree?
5   Why was the eagle seen as a problem child?
6   What was the point the author was trying to make in this story?
7   How do you define success?
8   What are your goals for your students?
9   How do we know the true potential of each student?
10 Where can we learn about each student's innate skills and talents, and how can we channel their energies in productive manners?
11 What do you plan on doing differently as a result of reading this story?

This powerful story can be viewed at www.raisingsmallsouls. com. I watched this video with my son Jake when he was in middle school. After watching the video, Jake turned to me and said, "I am the duck. I am good at math and need help in reading." I, too, had an "Aha moment" and realized that I was so focused on helping Jake improve in reading that I had failed to honor all of his other gifts. I was able to share my thoughts with him in what turned into a very emotional conversation for both of us. As a result we were able to enjoy a living amends by changing my behavior and focusing on his strengths.

I love to share this video when I do parenting workshops as well as youth leadership retreats. The self-awareness and clarity that comes as a result is profound.

By making the commitment each day to Honor your Spirit and the spirit of your students, you will surely see how it helps bring more joy, meaning and purpose back to teaching and learning, and honors the nobility in your students and yourself.

Nobility

Nobility is keeping faith with our true value as spiritual beings. It is living up to the virtues, the Divine trust within us. We treat ourselves and others with dignity and respect. We speak and act graciously. We choose the moral high road regardless of the cost. If others try to bring us down, we remain steadfast, remembering our true worth. Our sense of decency is our touchstone. The world's temptations cannot divert us from our purpose. We don't follow the path of least resistance. We lead principled lives. We live the good life.

The Virtues Project™

1   How are you, really?
2   How do you honor your spirit and the spirit of your students?
3   What brings you joy?

Chapter Nine

Just Listen: The Art of Companioning

"Listen"
by Dr. Ralph Roughton

When I ask you
To listen
And you start
Giving advice,
You have not done what I asked.

When I ask you
To listen
And you begin
To tell me why
I shouldn't feel the way I do,
You are trampling on my feelings.

When I ask you
To listen
And you feel
You have to do something to solve my problem,
You have failed me,
Strange as that may seem.

Listen.
All I asked you to do
Was listen,
Not talk,
Or do.
Just hear me.

I can do for myself:
I'm not helpless
Perhaps discouraged or faltering,
But not helpless.

When you do something for me
That I need to do for myself,
You contribute to my fear and weakness.
But, when you accept as a fact
That I feel what I feel,
No matter how irrational,
Then I can stop trying to convince you
And get on with understanding
What's behind that irrational feeling.

And, when that is clear,
The answers will be obvious,
And I won't need any Advice.

In Parker Palmer's book *The Courage to Teach – Exploring the Inner Landscape* of a *Teacher's Life*, he writes, "What does it mean to listen to a voice before it is spoken? It means making space for the other, being aware of the other, paying attention to the other, honoring the other. It means not rushing to fill our students' silences with fearful speech of our own and not trying to coerce them into saying the things that we want to hear. It means entering emphatically in to the student's world so that he or she perceives you as someone who is the promise of being able to hear another person's truth."

Have you ever had a bad day and you just wanted to come home and vent? And that caring person in the room offers you advice instead of an ear. How did that make you feel? Even though they are well intentioned, it often makes us feel angry, as if they do not believe that we are capable of solving our problems ourselves. Often times all we want is to be heard.

The Companioning Process is a seven step counseling technique that allows us to "listen" somebody into their own solution. Linda Kavelin-Popov, the founder of The Virtues Project, created this process when she was working with people who were dying; she was a spiritual caregiver in hospice.

What she realized is you cannot make somebody feel better when they are dying, but you can keep them company. Before I continue, think for a minute about the best listener that you know. What are those character qualities that they demonstrate?

A good listener makes eye contact with you, has positive body language, is open, and leans in when you are speaking. They give positive verbal signs with words like "yes," "uh-huh," and "I understand." They smile and show other positive facial expressions as well. They focus on you, do not interrupt what you say, and don't turn the conversation back onto themselves. They do not offer advice, they just simply listen.

Someone that is a poor listener does much the opposite. They might not give you eye contact, exhibit "closed" body language, or they might be doing other things. They might interrupt, change and steer the conversation so the focus is on them. Reflect for a moment. If "zero" is a poor listener and "ten" an excellent listener, where are you on that continuum?

Does it matter who you are listening to or the frame of mind you are in? If you are really frustrated, overwhelmed or in a rush, are you going to be able to be a good listener? If you are listening to somebody who is "sucking your energy dry" or pushes your buttons, are you able to be good a listener? There are so many different factors that influence our ability to be able to listen, including how we are physically feeling and if we are hungry or tired.

Part of the Companioning Process is to be able to discern when you are in that space where you can be an effective, caring and competent listener, and when you need to set a healthy boundary and let someone know that you do care about them but you are not in a place to hear them yet.

So what are the steps to the Companioning Process? First of all there are two over-arching virtues: compassion and detachment. You want to be able to put your shield of compassion on so that you can be there, you can walk along with that person and really let them feel that you care. The other virtue is detachment. You want to be able to be fully present and help lead them to their own solution, but you do not want to take on their pain or jump in to give them advice. Becoming detached allows the listener to use thinking and feeling to know when to be a guide and when just to listen.

As Douglas V. Stein says, "To listen another soul into a condition of disclosure and discovery may be almost the greatest service that any human being ever performs for another." That really does encapsulate the Companioning Process.

When someone comes to you and you see they are very excited or very upset, the first step is to open the door by asking, "What is happening?"

Step two is to basically close your mouth, open your heart and offer receptive silence. Now you are really receiving them fully and are listening with both your ears and your heart.

The third step is to ask "cup emptying" questions like "What was the hardest part?" or "What were you most angry about?" or "How did that make you feel?" We start those questions with "what" and "how," *never* "why," because "why" often puts people on to the defensive.

The fourth step is to look for sensory cues, to reflect on the feelings underneath their words. If you see somebody that is welling up with tears, ask "What are those tears for?" Asking this question gives the other person the opportunity and the permission to let those tears flow. It keeps them in their heart and not in their head. When we ask, "Why are you crying?" it takes them out of the emotion, and may even put them on the defensive.

After we focus on sensory cues, the fifth step is to ask virtues reflection questions. This is where we take the time to lead them in to their own solution. We might say "What virtue might be helpful?" or "What will give you the assertiveness to help you solve this problem?"

Once they focus and reflect on the virtue, the sixth step it to ask a "closure and integration" question like, "What is clearer to you now?" When we ask this question, it lets the person realize that they have come up with their own solution, not been given advice; it helps to strengthen their confidence and clarity.

Finally, the seventh step is to end with a virtues acknowledgement: "I really see your determination in working through this hard problem without giving up."

If these steps are too much to remember, just remember the first step and the last step. Ask what is happening, close your mouth, open your heart and listen, then offer a virtues acknowledgement. They will already feel more empowered than if someone just jumped in with advice.

I started using the companioning strategy when my kids were teenagers. It helped to transform our relationship, especially with my daughter who was 15 years old at the time. Although we had a strong relationship, she started shutting me out. Because I loved her and had been in similar circumstances as she was, I wanted to be loving and supportive and give her advice. But it backfired on me.

When I started using the Companioning Process she would come to me and share more and really open up, which helped to strengthen and unify our relationship.

My son was watching all this. Because he was on the other side of the Companioning Process, he became an extraordinary companioner himself. It was amazing how all of his friends would call and share what was going on in their hearts with him because he was such a good listener and companioned them to their own solutions without offering advice.

What does the Companioning Process look like in the classroom? Again when I was teaching kindergarten I had an experience where my little guy Thomas was over at the block center. It was time for us to transition and to go to P.E. When I asked everybody to clean up, Thomas started crying. Well, every early childhood educator knows that Thomas was crying because he did not want to stop playing with the blocks.

But instead of saying "Oh it is ok Thomas, you will have time to finish building after we are done with P.E.," I used the

Companioning Process with him. I said, "Thomas what is happening?" He said, "I do not want to go to P.E.." I said, "What is it about P.E. that is making you not want to go?" And then he said, "It is not that I do not want to go to P.E.; it is that I want to stay and build my blocks."

I said, "Honey what are those tears for?" As his tears were drying he said, "I really want to finish this project." I said, "Well, what virtue will help you to stop what you are doing now, get in line so we can be reliable and get to P.E. on time, and know that I will let you finish your building when we are done?" And he said with a quivering lip, "Flexibility." I said, "You know what sweetie, I really honor your flexibility and trust knowing that you will be able to finish your blocks when we come back."

What was really powerful is that it only took a minute; my other kids witnessed this so it helped to strengthen their trust in my ability to be there and care about what is important to them. It was also very different from other interactions that had happened in the past. Oftentimes when I would find myself in those rush situations I would panic. I realized I may have a student who was not cooperating because I did not give her the opportunity to share what was on her mind and heart.

Prior to learning about Companioning, you may have seen me coercing a five-year-old down the hall with arms and legs flailing and being followed by 25 other five-year-olds so we could get to
P.E. on time.

You can also Companion yourself. I had this experience the day I resigned from a job. I had come into the awareness that it was really time to leave this position and as I was driving home I was crying and I started Companioning myself.

"What is happening?" I asked myself. "What were the tears, what would give me the courage, what is clear to you now?" I gave myself a virtues acknowledgment and went through that whole reflective process. I was able to find the courage and integrity to leave a position that was no longer in alignment with my values.

What I probably found most surprising when using the Companioning Strategy is that it is powerful no matter who is on the other side. I have had the opportunity to Companion many grown men to tears. We would just be having a casual conversation, often about their children or their work and when we get to the heart of the matter, their eyes well up with tears. I ask them what the tears are for and then they start apologizing and saying, "I don't know, I don't know what is going on, this never happens to me, I am sorry, I am really embarrassed."

I let them know that it is the power of the Companioning strategy that helps them open up to clarity, and to find their own solution. Then we go through the rest of the steps where they are led to a powerful understanding at the end.

Even though the Companioning Process is simple, it is not easy. When I first used the Companioning Process I was a great companioner over the phone because I would have the list of the seven steps in front of me. I would also have a handout on how to Speak the Language of the Virtues and I would have a list of the virtues in front of me. If I was talking on the phone to a friend or colleague and I had to go through the Companioning Process, I could follow each step-by-step by looking at the sheet. I could also look at the list of virtues and match it back to how to Speak the Language and really be supportive to the person on the other line.

I also became comfortable with the Companioning Process when I would tuck my children in bed because, again, I had my helpful handouts posted where I could see them. I had the list of virtues and the Companioning Process on the wall right by their beds so when I was tucking them in we could have one of these heart-to-heart conversations at night.

I was not, however, very comfortable doing the Companioning Process at the beginning without my handouts. But, as with most things, the more I practiced the more comfortable I got. What I realized was it was not about being perfect in going through each step. What was most important was "wearing my shield of compassion and detachment" and being there to listen. Really listen, so they felt heard so loudly they could actually hear their own thoughts and come to their own clarity.

The Companioning Process is an empowering way to meet our needs to be seen, to be heard, to be taken seriously, to tell our stories and have them valued; to find meaning and purpose in what is happening, and to get to the heart of the matter. It is helpful when somebody has been sent to you for disciplinary action or has strong feelings and they are very sad, mad, glad, scared or confused; it is also valuable when they are having some kind of moral dilemma.

The Companioning Process is not about fixing, rescuing, curing, giving advice, sympathy, telling them what to do or being a victim. It is a walk along, coming from a place of respect, a caring presence, listening compassionately with detachment, asking 'how' and 'what 'questions. It comes from the virtues.

What is also essential when you are using the Companioning Process is the ability to respect and trust the wisdom that others have to solve their own problems. It is important to be open without an agenda so that we can be fully present to them.

Another powerful way of listening is by journaling. You can have your students journal as well. You can put a quote up on the board, read a virtues card or ask a question and give students the opportunity to go inside, be mindful of their own wisdom and write for clarity. Then give them the opportunity to share with another person or in a small group, and have other students give virtues acknowledgements so they feel seen, heard and witnessed.

Remember, the Companioning Process is not about giving advice, it is about being present.

Compassion

Compassion is deep empathy for another who is suffering or living with misfortune. It is understanding and caring, and a strong desire to ease their distress. Compassion flows freely from our hearts when we let go of judgments and seek to understand. Our compassionate presence helps people to know they are not alone. Sometimes they don't need us to fix anything. They only need to be heard with compassion, so that they can connect to their own inner wisdom. We need our own compassion as much as others do. Whether a silent prayer or a gentle touch, compassion is a priceless gift.

The Virtues Project

1 How well do you really listen, to yourself and to others?
2 Is there something that needs to be heard in any of your relationships?
3 Do you feel the need to fix and rescue when someone has a
   problem or do you trust the other person to solve it for himself or herself?

Chapter Ten

Windows to the World: Virtues Classrooms Around the Globe

"Our calling is where our deepest gladness and the world's hunger meet."

Frederick Buechner

The stories below are from fellow Virtues Project educators from around the world. They reflect different grade levels from six different countries and five regions in Canada. As you read them, I hope you will be inspired to become part of our Virtues Project global family and add your own story of transformation.

More Than Teaching Art, The Art of Teaching Reflections
By Kerry Tremblay, Master Facilitator, Singapore

I don't teach art to kids," a friend said to me as we shared a meal, "I teach kids through art."

I nodded thoughtfully, knowing that while I have a rigorous curriculum to deliver to my elementary students, I use that curriculum and the five simple strategies of The Virtues Project to help them become aware of their inherent virtues and their potential to develop and practice these virtues.

In the classroom, children are consistently and specifically acknowledged for practicing virtues such as honesty, reliability, self-discipline, kindness and patience. They are taught that life is about learning to develop these virtues in Teachable Moments. They are encouraged to look for and learn from Teachable Moments in their own lives and in the lives of others including historical figures and the characters in the literature we read. Clear classroom boundaries are created around virtues. Children are listened to and encouraged to reflect upon appropriate virtues when resolving conflicts and making decisions. Along the way, I believe that these students receive a powerful message. They learn to trust themselves and know intuitively that they will have the courage and integrity to meet the challenges they will inevitably face in life.

At the beginning of the year my students and I are detectives. In the classroom, I have a looking glass that reminds them that we are looking for the good in one another. Throughout the week children are acknowledged with WOW cards. WOW stands for "Watch out World" and the card says "I caught you practicing _____." The teacher or student writes the virtue they have seen the student practicing. These are deposited in a box throughout the week for a lucky draw in assembly. The child whose card is drawn receives 30 minutes of free time the following week for his entire class. At the end of each week, Virtues Ceremonies are special events in the classroom where children gather to acknowledge their peers verbally and with virtues vouchers for the virtues they have noticed in them. Children receive a virtues gem to remind them of the virtues they have practiced. These are lovingly stored in a special bag or decorated box. The children learn that they have all these virtues within them and that they can choose to act upon them in Teachable Moments. In our classroom we say, "Don't just know it, choose to show it."

Early in the year the children also decorate an empty Pringles Chips container to create Time Capsules. The time capsules include letters that both they and their parents write describing their hopes and fears for the year. They also identify the virtues that are strong within them and one virtue they would like to develop. When they open their capsules at the end of the year the children reflect upon how they have grown and changed. They usually discover that the fears they felt at the beginning of the year no longer exist. It is an opportunity for us as a learning community to celebrate the confidence each one has developed and to remind them to trust that they have within them the courage they will need to meet the challenges of the new academic year.

As one parent wrote to me at the end of the year: "Reading my time capsule letter I realize how important it was for him to secure some good and strong friends and while that has been a major achievement, I feel too that all your effort with the virtues has also rubbed off on my boy and he has a lot more inner codes to draw upon. Goodness knows he will need them."

Virtues education comes from the heart. Teachers too, must choose to learn about and develop their own virtues. We walk beside our students, listen to them, discern teachable moments in the classroom and share how we practice the virtues in our lives with truthfulness and humility.

There was one day when the class was almost ready to leave on a field trip. The girls were anxious about who they would be sitting with on the bus. I told them a story about my daughter when she was about the same age as they were now. She would sometimes become very upset and feel left out if she didn't get to sit beside a particular friend in class, or share a room with someone she chose on school camp. It left her feeling miserable. "Let's use our detachment and flexibility," I suggested. "How about we sit randomly on the bus and see if we can discover something new about somebody we don't usually spend time with? We can share what we have learned at the end of the trip and how we felt about the bus ride!"

As we walked to the bus I began chatting to one child about how much flexibility and detachment I had seen in her behavior throughout the year. I acknowledged her for her ability to work positively and cooperatively in most group situations.

"What helps you be so detached?" I asked with curiosity.

"Well the owl in the book I just read says it's okay if someone's behavior irritates you, Mrs. Tremblay, it's all about unconditional love."

As educators we know that children learn best in classrooms where there is a culture of respect and trust. The Virtues Project provides tools for teachers to create such a learning community. Virtues-based classrooms offer children clarity about who they really are. When children know that they have virtues within them and choose to use them they become empowered to live life confidently and with integrity.

Exploring a Culture of Character with Virtues and Values By Nigel Ipp (Nodi) B. Prim. Ed, B. Ed (UCT), Master Facilitator Virtues Project, South Africa

I was on an outing with my Lower Primary six to nine year olds from Riverlands School. We were visiting the New Maritime Museum in Fremantle, a double story building with giant, curving structures like sails, reminiscent of the Sydney Opera House. When we arrived on the second floor and stood in front of a giant window that stretched from floor to ceiling, I was surprised to see a boy holding back from the window. His Mum whispered to me, "Scared of heights." Later, the guide led the class across a decking section directly below the curving, sail-like roof. The boy stood back, alone. I knelt down beside him and said, "It's the way you think about it you know. Your fear of heights is real, but so is your knowledge of science. You know the builders would have made the floor safe for all the visitors to walk across it." He nodded silently. Then I asked, "Which part of your brain is going to win; the fearful part or the part that trusts in science? You can take my hand if you like and see how it feels." But I needn't have worried for he took a breath and strode off alone. It was a wonderful moment to be able to say to him, "I see your courage virtue has won my friend. You must be feeling really proud of yourself."

Later in the week I gave the boy the opportunity to pick the Virtue of the Week. He picked "Tact." This was quite amazing for there are 52 virtue cards and it was the third time in a month that "Tact" had been picked. The class discussed again how important tact is, for it's the way kind leaders include others and build trust in the group. The boy then picked another card from the virtue pack. It was "Consideration." Later, after discussing these virtues the boy came to me and expressed his wonder and appreciation. He was amazed that he had picked the two virtues that I had demonstrated earlier in the week to help him find courage and confidence. "Yes," I said, "In the past people may have teased you about your fear, but now we don't shame or frighten children when we help them overcome obstacles."

The 11th commandment – Evolve the Self By Nigel Ipp (Nodi) B. Prim. Ed, B. Ed (UCT), Master Facilitator Virtues Project, South Africa

When biology meets cooperation, integrity, respect and generosity, biology almost always wins. Let me illustrate with a student of mine whom I will call Evan. When I met him in pre-primary school he was as intense a boy as I had known. Later he was enrolled in my grade one and immediately set about finding his place in the pecking order of my Montessori-based grade 1-3 class. Within a short time he revealed his great skill in sports. He was totally absorbed by soccer and cricket and played them like his life was at stake. Fiercely competitive, determined and courageous to the point of recklessness, he would periodically find himself in front of me during break time telling me that nobody wanted to play with him. Upon my investigation it would always come down to Evan's intensity to win, score, dominate and overpower. Each time I would go through the sequence of thought that went something along these lines:

Me: What happened when the others stopped playing with you Evan?

Evan: Johnny got upset and shouted at me and wouldn't play and the others also stopped.

Me: Please get Johnny so we can hear the full story.

Evan: (fetches Johnny)

Me: Hi Johnny, I see you are upset. What happened?

Johnny: Evan kept taking the ball. He wouldn't pass. He shouted at me when I made a mistake. I got cross and picked up the ball and Evan shouted and kicked me. But Evan always wants the ball and wants to score and never passes.

Me: Okay thanks J, Evan what happened for you?

Evan: J always mucks up and I wanted to score and win and when I pass to him he mucks up so I just want to win the game. Me: But now there is no game to win is there Evan?

Evan: No!

Me: Seems like the others are upset with you again.

Evan: Yes! Me: Okay, let's go through it again my friend. I want to remind you about what I have told you before – you know, how good you are at soccer. You are one of the best I have ever seen at your age. You kick with both feet, you are enthusiastic, you love the game and your determination to win is very powerful. These virtues will be your great strength through life. But if you forget to include other virtues in your mix, then your strengths will also be your biggest challenge. Which virtues can you add into your mix so that the other children don't get hurt and want to stop playing with you?

Evan: Respect.

Me: Yes and…

Evan: Consideration.

Me: Good, you've remembered them now. I'd like to add in patience and tolerance, because each person is different and has a different set of gifts. Yours is soccer, but if you can't be a team player, then you can't win either, because being a team player is about including everyone and sometimes it can even lead to losing, which is also about character building. So patience allows you to take turns and share while tolerance allows you to respect that each of you are different and have different skills and abilities.

Evan: Yes…

After some more clarifying of the situation, I get the boys to shake hands and invite Evan to remember to respect his team and include them so that they enjoy playing with him and being in his team because he is so good. I then remind him that this strong set of skills are likely to overpower him again and again, but that with support from the boys, my understanding and his commitment to calling on the other virtues of "inclusion," in time this intention of his might come to the fore, resulting in less difficulties and more fun.

Here we see how Evan's particular genetic make up, his biology, dominates and almost always wins. This kind of boy would, without the scaffolding and nurture of a supportive and effective adult, become more and more alienated and even likely become a bully with many conflict situations in his life, leading through to adulthood.

As a result of the kind of intervention I made in his young life, he had the opportunity to put his particular character strengths to the most effective use. He was not vilified, rather he was supported. He was not told how badly behaved he was, rather his strong traits that led to his conflict were framed in the positive light that they deserved. The gift that Evan got was the opportunity to Evolve Himself and the continual reminder, often daily, that he needs to respect the rights of others, since those values mean that his rights are also respected. The ways in which I tried to help Evan place respect and peacefulness first were many and varied, and sometimes it felt like we'd never get there. But his human right was to have me do that for him. The effect of this kind of intervention was highly prized by his family, who did their best to support the process. Evan is now a fairly stable settled boy and he and his family remain appreciative years later for the compassionate and caring interventions I offered in the tender and impressionable years of the Foundation Phase of his learning. He remains a powerful, enthusiastic, courageous boy whose favorite virtue is determination. And I am sure his growth virtues (not weakness) will remain a growth for the rest of his life, but he has been given the knowledge and the opportunity to Evolve Himself so that he is less dominated by his genetic make up. It is not an 'either or' approach to evolving the self, to resolving conflict, it's an 'and with' approach. We built on to his character instead of undermining it or attempting to crush it. Not only did we build on to his character, we actually celebrated and acknowledged the very qualities that led to the conflict, for they are genuinely the qualities or virtues that will lead him to success in his life.

Evan's instincts for survival were so powerful that his behavior was dominated by them. This is common for young children, let alone teenagers and adults. Biology would have won out and perpetuated the conflict competitive experience that dominated the human species. As can be seen from this example though, there are ways to make a difference if we take the idea of human rights and human responsibilities and put them both at the top of our pile of values. Then we too are called to evolve ourself, for we too grow in understanding, patience, tenderness and respect.

My Favorite School Story is the Virtues in Chicken Soup By Betty Doughtery, Master Facilitator, Victoria Canada, BC

With some trepidation, I started reading a *Chicken Soup* story to my junior high math classes (grades 8 - 1) every Thursday. My son told me I would get laughed out of school but my passion as a teacher was always to inspire the children to be the best they could be with every means available including Brain Gym, the importance of water and good nutrition, and study skills. I have always loved a good story, finding it an excellent way to connect with people of all ages and so, one day, near the end of class I read them a story. "Why do we have to listen to stories in math class?" they wanted to know. "This isn't English!" I explained that I wanted to teach about life, not just math.

Math was important and I loved teaching it but developing perseverance, caring, respect, courtesy, and the courage to make good choices for themselves and others was even more important. I invited them to write reflections on the stories, what they learned from them and turn them in if they wanted to. I read them stories about taking responsibility, being accountable, standing up for the underdog, the courage to dream big and make it come true, how easily and unknowingly we can avert suicide just by befriending someone who looks lost and alone. By the end of the month if it looked like I wasn't going to have time to read a story, someone would put their hand up and ask for a story. They wrote me all kinds of notes from decisions to be more compassionate themselves to stories of abuse in their own homes. I referred several to the counselors for help. I encouraged them on special occasions (birthdays, Christmas, Valentine's Day, Thanksgiving) to write notes to people letting them know the difference they had made. I have a whole file of notes they wrote to me appreciating this added dimension to their learning. By the end of the year, rapport in the classroom was such that I wrote them a class letter, a sort of written commencement address encouraging them to continue the process of becoming the best they can be for the rest of their lives and gave each of them a blue ribbon that said "Who I Am Makes A Difference" (see the original Chicken Soup for the Soul story by Helice Bridges of that title). I knew I had found my niche when the student body's Santa presented me with a can of Chicken Soup at the Christmas assembly before the break. This was before I knew anything about The Virtue Project, but it was my segue into their lives to work The Five Strategies with them and call them to their virtues.

Transformation of Huntington Hills School By Donna Wheatcroft, Master Facilitator, Alberta Canada

Preamble: From the Huntington Hills School the principal and his Parent Council President attended a two-day workshop. Then on a PD Day he came back and brought 1/3 of his staff to a two-hour workshop. In the fall I did a full day workshop with the whole staff, a three-evening (six-hour) workshop with the parents and five days in the school doing virtues activities with the students and teacher in the classroom, and five noon hours with the principal and his volunteer leadership group. Because of the unity, commitment, purposefulness and enthusiasm from the staff and parents, results/outcomes were a change in climate to more peacefulness (safer, less stress), reduced violence, increase in student enrollment and morale. A school about to be closed now had a waiting list of 90 students as a result of the staff committed to implementing The Virtues Project.

The Calgary Herald reported: Principal's hair, fights both missing at Huntington Hills Calgary Herald; Calgary, Alta.; Jun

12, 2003; Graeme Morton; Full Text: (Copyright Calgary Herald 2003.)

If only feuding world leaders could take a chapter from the book of the students at Huntington Hills Elementary . . .

"When I first came here a couple of years ago, I thought it was an excellent school. But we started to keep close track of the numbers and found we'd had 55 fights in that school year. We as a staff knew we could do better," principal Gord Aldridge recalls.

"We started a conscious effort to talk to our children about alternatives to settling problems by acting like a bully or by starting fights. In subsequent years, we went down to 22 fights, then to 11 last year. In September, we challenged the kids to see if we could go an entire year without a fight. I asked them what prize they'd like at the end of the year and they said they wanted me to shave my head," says Aldridge.

Last Friday, the students got their wish as Aldridge's head became a "hair-free zone" at the hands of some of his delighted staff members.

Key elements to the turnaround at Huntington Hills include a Dare-to-Care project, which examines the causes of bullying and how to combat it, and a program called The Virtues Project, which promotes such qualities as honesty, empathy, respect and open-mindedness.

"From Day One in September, we stressed these issues in our daily announcements, we asked the kids what virtue they were practicing today, we started singing 'O Canada' every week," says Aldridge. Grade 5 and 6 students at Huntington Hills have taken on leadership roles among their peers. "When new children move into the school, the older students make sure they're aware that we just don't fight at Huntington Hills," Aldridge says.

Despite having a student population of only about 200, Huntington Hills has raised more than $2,000 this year for humanitarian efforts in Iraq. Photos of students proudly perched on the principal's motorcycle were hot sellers.

Kathy Nourse, the president of the school's parent's council, says the entire Huntington Hills community has bought into the program. "A couple of years ago, we were one of the schools that was seriously considered to be closed under the LEAP process," says Nourse.

"Morale was definitely down. We wanted to look at ways to make our school stand out, to make it an attractive place to come to. "We've had workshops with the parents on the goals of the Virtues program to make sure they're being reinforced at home. Now, we're hearing from the kids that they think Huntington Hills is a much safer, less stressful place to attend," says Nourse. "It's been a really dramatic turnaround. Now we have students enrolled in our school from other areas and there are waiting lists for certain grades."

A school wide celebration of their fight-free year will be held on the final day of classes, June 26.

The Name Caller, Virtues in the Middle School By Sharon Mann, USA

The behavior of a student in our middle school was brought to my attention by my paraprofessionals. They observed "Tom" calling female students by derogatory names which were based on negative physical attributes. Tom was in a nine-week class I was teaching and I was just getting to know him when another student told me that he had called her a racist name. I felt that an intervention was needed and that the whole class would participate.

I introduced the next class with an anti-bullying survey. Students were put into preselected groups of four to talk about and answer the questions on the survey which addressed bullying issues in the school and their personal opinions on bullies which included adult interventions, student interventions, and a self-evaluation of bullying behaviors. The students were very cooperative and expressed appreciation for the opportunity to voice their opinions. Upon collecting the surveys I told the students that I would tally the results and share them at the next class.

The next day I brought in the classroom poster of the Virtues: The Gifts of Character and gave each student a copy of the results, which were brutally honest and illuminating. They were then asked to write down whether they believed that interventions by teachers and students were effective. Using the Gifts of Character poster they were then to list at least five (out of 15 or more) virtues the bully needed, five (out of 15 or more) the bystander needed, and at least three that the victim needed.

As I was walking down the aisles talking with individual students about their bullying experiences and what virtues might be used, I came upon Tom, who was conscientiously answering the questions. He admitted to me that he was a bully and when I asked him what virtue he might need to work on, he studied the poster for some time and then answered, "Tolerance." I acknowledged him for his honesty and clarity and expressed my confidence that he would learn to practice tolerance.

The whole class became closer as a result of this exercise and name-calling by Tom was no longer an issue.

In addition to using virtues during Teachable Moments, I have tried to look carefully at each student to find their hidden gems so that I can sincerely describe them on report cards and progress reports. I believe it is important that the student knows that "I see them." On one report card I wrote that the student was diligent and respectful and a joy to have in class. The next time I saw her, she ran up to me with a big smile and said how pleased she was to know that she brought me joy! She thought it was a joke but I assured her it was true. She remained respectful and joyful towards me even though I only taught her for nine weeks.

Story of Determination By Verónica Isabel Tróchez, Master Facilitator of The Virtues Project™ in Honduras

I did some voluntary work at my son´s school, facilitating a two-day introductory workshop of The Virtues Project™ to all the teachers, right before the school year started.

By the end of the workshop the principal of the school suggested that they make a Virtues Pick every month and work on that virtue for a whole month with the children. So the first pick was made right away and "determination" appeared.

We read the concepts for that virtue and I asked them for ideas on how to teach determination to the students. Many creative ideas arose. After a while, one of the teachers raised her hand with a clearly worried expressed: "How will I teach the concept of determination to my children? They are the pre-kinder students! Determination is such a long word and its meaning is so complex."

Grace brought me into discernment and I responded: "Trust that they will learn it. Talk about determination, how you practice it, acknowledge yourself out loud when you practice determination, acknowledge them when you see them practicing determination as well."

About two months later, a lady approached me and asked me: "Have you been teaching virtues in the classrooms?" I answered with a surprising "No," wondering what that question was about. When I asked her what had made her believe that, she replied: "My daughter told me the other day: Mom, you should use your determination and finish what you start!"

I smiled full of joy, remembering that that had been our Virtues Pick for the first month of school.

I asked her: "And how old is your daughter?"

"Four" she answered. "She is in pre-kinder."

My joy was doubled! After our talk, I ran to find the pre-kinder teacher to acknowledge her for her determination, purposeful commitment and perseverance!

A Lovely Discovery

I taught Biology class to a group of 10 students from Tenth grade during a school year. Every Monday we would make a Virtues Pick and one of the students would read the card aloud. Some of them would briefly share an experience on the virtue they picked. We did not have much time for that as the contents of the subject being studied were big and we could hardly use our time in other matters. Still I was committed to share the virtues with my 10 students.

Sometimes I would forget the Virtues Pick and there was always someone to remind me to do so, just before I left the class-room, so we would do it real fast.

By the end of the school year, when they wrote their final exam, I included a question: "What did you learn this year during the Biology class?" Most of the students answered: "I learned about the cell, Krebs's cycle, photosynthesis, ecosystems, etc."

One student, who had not been very committed to hand in his homework throughout the school year, and with whom I had to speak on several occasions, companioning him and encouraging him to show me his steadfastness, resolution and dedication, wrote the following: "I learned during this year to find the best of me. You showed me that I can do many things if I commit myself to do so. I learned that I have all the virtues inside and that I am a good person."

That meant so much to me and I am certain that no matter if it is a "high or a small dose of virtues," their effect can fill you with awe.

Caution: Do not consult a physician if you have side effects with the use of the virtues!
Mushuau Innu First Nations School in Natuashish, By Bob Jackman, Newfoundland and Labrador, Canada

Natuashish, NL is a First Nations school with approximately 400 students on the North Coast of Labrador. The Innu had just taken over their school and they were going to be developing a new curriculum for their school. I was excited to be part of it. However, from the moment I arrived I realized that something was not right. Firstly, no new curriculum was being developed and the discipline policy had all but been removed from the school. Students faced no consequences for their actions. Art, gym, music, outings, suspensions, detentions, etc., could not be used for deterrents to get students to work and behave appropriately.

Fortunately, I had a copy of the *Virtues Project Educators Guide* and the *Family Virtues Guide* with me and I began right away to teach the virtues to my class of grade six's. We looked at what the virtue was, how to practice it, why practice it and how to look for the signs of success. We had a virtue of the week and would keep an eye on who was practicing the virtue. We also kept a wall decoration of the virtues we learned. I began by giving each student an old penny. I kept a shiny new one for myself. I asked them if their old penny was ever as new as the one I had. Yes, of course they said and proceeded to tell me how their penny became so dirty. I then asked them if the dirty penny could become shiny again and they said yes and came up with various ways to do this. During the activity I had one student come to me and say, "Look sir, it's gettin' new again; but, it's hard work though!" At this point I introduced the idea that a new born baby is so precious, clean and brand new just like the penny was. I asked the class about what could happen to the baby as it grows up to become a teenager to cause it to no longer shine as bright. You'd be surprised at some of the things they tell you that the baby goes through that causes it to no longer shine as nice as it did as a baby. (Alcoholic parents don't care about them, sexual assaults, hanging out with a group that continues to break the law, being bullied at school and on Facebook, etc.) But can the stuff that keeps the grown baby from continuing to shine be cleaned away similarly to what we did with the penny?

I quickly realized that this was having a major impact on my class. They began to become much more controlled and I was, for the most part, able to get them to do the required material/ activities for the day. I had a teacher ask me what I was doing in my classroom because whatever it was he wanted to do it too. He said that I had the best class in the building. It was flattering but I knew that The Virtues Project was the key and it is extremely important to have a dedicated staff. I lent the books I had to another teacher who had the same results with her class as I did. She was also asked by other teachers about what she was doing in her class to get them to behave so well.

Because of the success I was having with The Virtues Project, I decided to do a proposal to the Innu School Board for funding to bring a facilitator to Natuashish to introduce it to the rest of the staff. It was readily accepted and Ms. Donna Wheatcroft from Calgary, Alberta arrived in Natuashish for a two-day in-service for all staff at the end of August 2010. As of May 2012, the Educator's Guides and cards are being used by teachers. The coordinator that visits the school on a regular basis said that there is a gradual increase in virtuous behavior in the school.

The Power of the Can By Barry Lewis Green, The Unity Guy™, Master Facilitator – Halifax, Canada

A number of years ago, I found myself conducting a two-day program around leadership. This was no ordinary program or ordinary group. They never are. Still, what made this group "special" were its nature and its place and its reason for being.

Within this group were 10 youth; remarkable youth, but then they all are. These youth had been known to be "at risk" or "at promise." I simply say that they were "at something." Suffice it to say that they were a group of youth ages 18-22 who had had their own challenges in life, myriad and many in some cases. They all lived within a block or so, within a low income neighborhood that had gained its own name within the city. And these youth were the heirs of that name.

The two days were to be about personal leadership; the kind of leadership that says I count, I matter, and I have a voice and something to contribute. These two days were infused with my own body of work around leadership and The Five Strategies of The Virtues Project™, in which I believe so heartily.

After one day, we had built a real collective relationship, having fun with the material and getting to know each other in the most cool of ways. I had addressed what I call the Seven L's of Leadership and we were building a strong and cohesive experience together.

When the second day came, I knew that I planned a classic spirit walk for the youth, just before lunch. I also realized that the neighborhood in which we found ourselves, including the community center in which the training was being conducted, was, in spite of many efforts to beautify, lacking in nature. There was much brick and mortar, little in the way of trees and grass. Still, hoping that being brazen and bold were virtuous... I say audacious... I set out to assign the spirit walk, not knowing what would come of it.

Would the youth find any nature to which to relate. Would they walk separately or hang? Would they find it odd and weird? Was this something that they may opt out of, despite our bonding and trust?

Well, 30 minutes before lunch, they returned; and return they did. We had the opportunity to go around the room and ask each youth what they had found and share the quality or virtue of which it spoke to them. There were blades of grass, and sticks, and rocks, and more. But it was the last youth who more than astounded me.

This youth was about six feet tall; with a bright white 05 basketball shirt, earrings, tattoos, shaved head, and ball cap with brim off to the side. He had the bling, all of it. He had a countenance that said "don't mess with me" but not in an overtly aggressive way.

I was curious. What had he found? So, it was his turn and I turned the floor over to him.

From his deep pocket he drew out a crushed pop can. I mean it was crushed, flattened, run over. It was flat and dirty. Now, I was more than curious. I said, "What is it"? He told us, and described it as I have done so here. He said, "This can is crushed, spat on, kicked around, discarded, beaten down... but it's still here." Even as I write this, I am moved. We all were. He knew not yet the virtue by name, but he knew it by nature. When I said to him, "You are speaking of resilience." He showed a smile as if to say "Yeah, I am." I smile when I think about it.

This youth was the champion of resilience; its standard bearer. Still, I am reminded that youth typically are, and we need that virtue in these days of great change. I had spent two days with a remarkable group of young people, supposedly showing them the path to leadership. Instead, they showed me our greatest path.

The Healing Power of Virtues By Val Hilliker, Virtues Project
Master Facilitator, World Laughter Leader, Central Alberta
www.valhilliker.com

This was an amazing experience showing that the virtue words are power filled. A grade three student who hadn't spoken in two years is now speaking to her classmates and teacher. Her volunteering to assist in my show triggered the change.

I used this child for the remote magic drawing board bit, where I turn the child into the star. It is all because of them that the board comes to life. I asked for a volunteer who had courage as their core virtue and her hand went up. I always ask the teachers to choose the student but this time they wanted me to do that and insisted in me choosing the one who hadn't spoken in two years - the teachers were dancing wildly in the back of the gym and pointing to her.

As the child volunteer approached me she walked up to the front with trepidation. I knew we had to encourage and awaken her courage. I asked her to take a deep breath in and then I said I see you are courageous. I get the student to draw the nose and straight line then later in the show when it springs to life I let the student take the credit for its animation. I said to the child volunteer, you are going to have to bring a pen at recess and sign autographs and let your classmates know how that worked. She did just that. It was one of those moments that I will never forget. Her first bow was hard for her to do so I got the audience to really encourage her and as she bowed I threw the pupils in the puppets eyes and then removed them so she didn't see them go in. I do this three times and her bows to the appreciative audience got very strong. Her classmates knew how hard this was for her and I saw and recognized the improvement by commenting on her courage.

Now her courage and voice is awakened. I believe I was just at the right place at the right time with the right words and a way to use them to awaken her courage. It had nothing to do with me and everything to do with the board, message, the virtue word courage and she was ready to break loose.

In no way am I taking credit for something that happened, just enjoying the magical awe-filled virtues moment.

A Story of a Boy Bullied for One Year as a Ninth Grader Shared by Hiroshi Ohuchi, Master Facilitator from Yamanashi, Japan

This essay was written by a 20-year-old university freshman. One of the crucial cultural notes is that every Japanese celebrates his/her "Coming of Age Day" during the first week or so of January. They return to their hometowns and usually get together with the high school young people they grew up with. They wear formal kimono (men and women) and there are speeches by the mayor and others and congratulations all around. It is often the first time they see the friends they went to high school with, after two years of university life or life working in a job. So, as in this story, it can be a great source of anxiety or joy...

When I was a child, I was a coward and had no confidence. I had various complexes. I was pretty good at studying but I was very bad at sports. On top of that, I was very shy so I had few friends and most of the time I spent by myself. My elder sister, seven years older, was a tomboy and very friendly. She was popular at school and in the neighborhood. My younger sister, three years younger than I, was very free-spirited and she had a personality which attracted people to her. I was envious of both sisters. I wondered how this kind of difference comes about even though we were brother and sister.

Because of this personality I had and my poor social skills, many problems occurred when I became a junior high school kid. I didn't want problems, but somehow troubles kept happening in my relationships with others. I cursed, deeply, this personality of mine. In those days I really hated myself.

When I became a ninth grader it began. Probably it was due to my personality but it was so painful and tough. I almost wanted to kill myself. From that spring on, for one year, until I graduated, I was severely bullied by a group of classmates. It was a very cruel thing, like those depicted in T.V. dramas. My desk, my locker, my shoebox became like their trash box. Whenever they found time for it they took me to the back of the school building and beat me up like a punching bag. My body had bruises all over the place and I did my best to hide them from my family. "Why me?" I kept asking myself. I knew that my personality probably was the cause, but it was too cruel. I didn't want to hurt them in any way and I wanted to become friends with them. These painful and sad feelings gradually turned into a strong hatred toward the bullies. This bullying continued for one year until I graduated from junior high school.

After graduation, the bullies went to a less than average high school outside the city and I went to a better public high school from which most grads go on to university. Thus, we moved away from each other where we didn't have to see each other. In this way the bullying stopped, but the experience left a very deep scar in me. From then on, the only reason I found for living was to get revenge.

"Revenge," meaning I wanted to become a better human being than they. So, every day I thought of how to get revenge in that way. I challenged myself to try many things. I participated in various sports activities and volunteered for many things. I was completely different from my old self. Thanks to that, I acquired a lot of knowledge and skills and my talent began to bloom in various ways.

But at the bottom of my heart I was feeling empty because all of this was motivated by that negative experience. In the end, I felt that my wounded heart could only be healed by other's hearts (note: meaning "other people's friendship"). So, in spite of all these accomplishments, I was dissatisfied in my life. I went to a university in Tokyo and left behind those bad memories in my hometown. However, even after I entered university, my past persistently lingered around me.

Then I became Mr. Ohuchi's seminar student. And there I was taught The Virtues Project. In this class I thought about many virtues and in the process of sharing with many other students I felt that my empty heart began to fill with a new life force. Trying to make myself understood, trying to choose words so that the other person could understand me, choosing words carefully to express who I am...I came to know who I am and found some unknown aspects of myself. In this process I began to realize what I want to think, what I want to see and what I want to do in my life. I realized I was beginning to forgive the past. When I was acknowledged by others in the process of sharing, it was like a time of miraculous healing because my whole life I was hardly ever acknowledged for my goodness. I said, "The human heart can be nurtured only by other human being's hearts." This acknowledgment of my virtues by others brought me that human warmth which I had forgotten, triggered by the bullying, and which I had been seeking.

January 2006. Ceremony for Becoming an Adult
The Adult Day Ceremony was to be held in my hometown (for all 20-year-olds.) "If I go to this ceremony, I will meet the group of boys who bullied me, for the first time in five years." At first, I was really scared. For one thing, I was afraid of them. And even more, I was afraid that my heart, which was beginning to forgive them, would turn to hatred again. But I went. I saw them. When I talked to the guy who was the leader of the bullies, he quietly accepted me and then he apologized to me deeply, from the bottom of his heart. I also was able to accept his apology from the bottom of my heart. I forgave him. I forgave them. At this moment, my five year journey of pain ended.

During the The Virtues Project Class, Mr. Ohuchi said, "Of all the virtues, the virtue of forgiveness may be the most difficult to practice." In fact, I spent many years in pain before I was able to forgive the bullies.

One thing I came to realize from this experience is that people want to forgive at the bottom of their being, even when they say they hate someone and will never forgive them, because it is very painful and takes a lot of energy to live hating someone. For me, I gained new strength and the power to live when I forgave. Yes, to practice the virtue of forgiveness is not easy, but whoever is in pain and in the midst of hatred, in fact it is they who want to forgive. I declare, "The forgiving mind opens a new path." I declare, "I am newly born here."

Hope

Hope is looking to the future with trust and faith. It is optimism in the face of adversity. Without hope, we lose our will to live fully. Hope gives us the courage to keep moving forward. It can be elusive when we have suffered often, yet it is the light that can redeem our dreams. With hope, we know we are not alone. There is always help when we are willing to ask. There are gifts to be gleaned from all that happens. With hope, we find the confidence to try and try again.

The Virtues Project™

1 How have you witnessed virtues making a difference?
2 What will your virtues story be?
3 What legacy do you wish to leave?

Epilogue

As this book was heading toward publication, a great tragedy took place in Newtown, Connecticut on December 14, 2012. Twenty innocent first grade students, four dedicated teachers, two courageous administrators, a mother and a son were killed in a heartbreaking shooting at Sandy Hook Elementary School. Though devastated by their loss, the community came together in unity to share their commitment to preventing tragedies like this from ever happening again. They did not ask for more police support, surveillance cameras, metal detectors or that educators get trained on how to use guns. Instead, they reminded us of the power of the human spirit and that when people pull together in unity that good can come from tragedy, hope from despair. God bless the souls who died and the ones who carry on. Let the words below be the reminder we need to be resilient and commit to bringing joy, meaning and purpose back to teaching and learning.

The Sandy Hook PROMISE
www.sandyhookpromise.org

This is a Promise
That even though hearts are broken; Our spirit is not.
And it is with this knowledge that we are able to move forward with purpose...and strength...
This is a Promise we make to our precious children To support our own, our families, our neighbors, and our teachers, with dedication, love and community because every human being is filled with incredible potential to create positive change.

This is a Promise
To honor the lives lost by creating timeless change from the moment of violence. To choose love, belief and hope, not anger when our hearts are filled with unbearable pain.

This is a Promise
To be open to all possibilities. To seek no agenda other than to make our community and our nation a safer, happier place.

This is a Promise
To do everything in our power to be remembered, not as a town filled with grief and victims but as the place where real change began.

This is a Promise
To have conversations on ALL the issues. Conversations where listening is as important as speaking. Conversations where even those with the most opposing views can debate with good will.

This is THE Promise
That we'll turn those conversations into actions. You and me. We are Sandy Hook. This is our promise. To choose love, and to love everyone, and to start now.

Love

Love is at the center of our being. It is the vital force that gives us energy and direction. It connects one heart with another. Love is irresistible attraction and affection for a person, a place, an idea, or even for life itself. Love is cherishing others, treating them with tenderness. Love thrives on acceptance and appreciation. It has the power to heal. It calls us to continually hone ourselves, while releasing the need to control or make someone in our image. Nurtured by commitment and seasoned by kindness, love is our greatest gift.

The Virtues Project™

References and Recommended Reading

One of the reasons I chose to write this book was to share the wisdom I have gleaned from reading the authors listed below. I encourage you to add their work to your library. Enjoy!

Abrams, H. & Giller, D. (n.d.). *I'm a person.* Retrieved August 2006 from www.iamaperson.com.

Abrams, J. (2009). *Having hard conversations.* Thousand Oaks, CA: Corwin.

Byrne, R. (2006). *The secret.* New York: ATRIA Books.

Canfield, J., & Hanson, M. V. (1993). *Chicken soup for the soul: 101 Stories to open the heart and rekindle the spirit.* Deerfield Beach, FL: Health Communications, Inc.

Canfield, J., & Switzer, J. (2005). *The success principles: How to get from where you are to where you want to be.* New York: William Morrow.

Collins, J. (2001). *Good to great.* New York: Harper Collins.

Covey, S. (1989). *The seven habits of highly effective people.* New York: RosettaBooks, LLC.

Curwin, R. L., Mendler, A. M., & Mendler, B. D. (2008). *Discipline with dignity: New challenges for new solutions.* Alexandria, VA: Association for Supervision and Curriculum Development.

Dweck, C.S. (2006). *Mindset: The new psychology of success.* New York: HarperCollins.

Dyer, W. (2006). *Inspiration: Your ultimate calling.* Carlsbad, CA: Hay House.

Elias, M. J., Zins, J. E., Weissberg, R. P., Frey, K.S., Greenberg, M. T., Haynes, N. M., Kessler, R., Schwab-Stone, M. E., & Shriver, T. P. (1997). *Promoting social and emotional learning: Guidelines for educators.* Alexandria, VA: Association for Supervision and Curriculum Development.

Emerzin, M., & Bozza, K. (2007). *Every monday matters: 52 ways to make a difference.* Nashville, TN: Thomas Nelson, Inc.

Emoto, M. (2004). *Hidden messages in water.* Hillsboro, OR: Beyond Words Publishing.

Eyler, J. & Giles, D. E. (1999). *Where's the learning in service learning.* San Francisco: Jossey-Bass.

Gartrell, D. (2003). *The power of guidance: Teaching social/emotional skills in early childhood classroom.* Washington, DC: NAEYC.

Goleman, D. (1995). *Emotional intelligences: Why it can matter more than IQ.* New york: Bantam.

Greenwald, R. Z., *Animal school.* Retrieved November 24, 2006, from http://raisingsmallsouls.com/animal-school-video-inspires-individuality-acceptance/.

Gruwell, E. (1999). The freedom writers diary: How a teacher and 150 teens used writing to change themselves and the world around them. New York: Broadway Books.

Hawkins, D. (1995). *Power vs force: The hidden determinants of human behavior.* Carlsbad, CA: Hay House, Inc.

iEARN. Retrieved on December 17, 1997 from http://iEarn.org.

Jensen, E. (2008). *Brain based learning: The paradigm of teaching.* Thousand Oaks, CA: Corwin.

Kavelin-Popov, L. (2000). *The virtues project educator's guide: Simple ways to create a culture of character.* CA: Jalmar Press.

Kavelin-Popov, L. (2004). *A pace of grace: Virtues for a sustainable life.* New York: Plume.

Kavelin-Popov, L., Popov, D., & Kavelin, J. (1997). *The family virtues guide: Simple ways to bring out the best in our children and ourselves.* New York: Plume.

Kessler, R. (2000). *The soul of education: Helping students find connection, compassion and character in school.* Alexandria, VA: Association for Supervision and Curriculum Development.

Knight, J. (2011). *Unmistakable impact: A partnership approach for drastically improving instruction.* Thousand Oaks, CA: Corwin.

Konner, M. (1993). *Childhood, and a multi-cultural view.* New York: Little Brown & Co.

Leonsis, T. (2010). *The business of happiness: 6 secrets to extraordinary success in work and in life.* Washington, D.C.: Regnery Publishing, Inc.

Lickona, T. (2004). *Character Matters: How to help our children develop good judgment, integrity, and other essential virtues.* New York: Touchstone.

Lickona, T., & Davidson, M. (2005). *Smart and good high schools: Integrating excellence and ethics for success in school, work and beyond.* Cortland, NY: Center for the 4th and 5th Rs / Washington, DC: Character Education Partnership.

Marshall, S. P. & Price, H.B. (2007). *The learning compact redefined: A call to action.* Alexandria, VA: Association for Supervision and Curriculum Development.

Merton, R. K. (1949). *Social theory and social structure.* New York: Free Press.

Mogul, W. (2001). *The blessing of a skinned knee: Using jewish teaching to raise self- resilient children.* New York: Penguin Compass.

My Hero Project. The heroic virtues forum. Retrieved November 19, 2011 from http://myhero.com/go/forum/.

Palmer, P. (1998). *The courage to teach: exploring the inner landscape of a teacher's life.* San Francisco: Jossey-Bass.

Parr, T. (2001). *It's ok to be different.* New York: Little Brown Books for Young Readers.

Pink, D. (2005). *A whole new mind: Why the right brainer will rule the future.* New York; Riverhead Books.

Pink, D. (2009). *Drive: The surprising truth about what motivates us.* New York: Riverhead Books.

Quinn, G. H. (1995). *365 Meditations for teachers.* New York: Scholastic.

Rath, T., & Clifton, C (2004). *How full is your bucket?* New York: Gallup Press.

Ridnouer, K. (2006). *Managing your classroom with heart : A guide to nourishing adolescent learners.* Alexandria, VA: Association for Supervision and Curriculum Development.

Seligman, M. E. (1990). *Learned optimism: How to change your mind and your life.* New York: Pocket Books.

Seligman, M. E. (2003). *Authentic happiness: Using the new positive psychology to realize your potential for deep fulfillment.* London: Nicholas Brealey Publishing.

Solo, B., (2007). *Activating the desire to learn.* Alexandria, VA: Association for Supervision and Curriculum Development.

Sornson, R. & Scott, J. (1997). *Teaching and joy.* Alexandria, VA: Association for Supervision and Curriculum Development.

Stepanek, M. J. T. (2002). *Hope through heartsongs.* New York: Hyperion.

Styles, D. (2001). *Class meetings: Building leadership, problem solving and decision making skills in the respectful classroom.* Markham, ON: Pembroke.

Sutton, R. (2007). *The no asshole rule: Building a civilized workplace and surviving one that isn't.* New York: Hachette Book Group.

Tally, B. (2008). *Tally Up – The Excitement of Value Based Living.* Germantown, MD: TalleY Up Press.

The Advancement Project & Power You Center for Social Change (2011). *Telling it like it is: youth speak out on the school to prison pipeline.* Washington, D.C./ Miami, FL.

Tough, P. (2012). *How children succeed: Grit, curiosity and the hidden power of character.* Boston: Houghton Mifflin Harcourt.

Tracy, D. (2002) *Blue's clues for success: The eight secrets behind a phenomenal business.* Chicago: Dearborn Trade Books.

Urban, H. (2004). *Life's great lessons* and *positive words, powerful results – Simple ways to honor, affirm* and *celebrate life.* New York: Fireside.

Walsch, N. D. (1998). *The little soul and the sun: A children's parable adapted from conversations with god. Charlottesville, VA:* Hampton Roads Publishing Company, Inc.

Wheatley, M. J. (2010). *Perseverence.* San Francisco: Berrett-Koehler Publishers, Inc.

Wholey, D. *(2007) This is america:* Washington, DC: Dennis Wholey Enterprises.

Wood, J. (2007). *Yardsticks: Children in the classroom ages 4 to 14, a resource for parents and teachers.* Turners Falls, MA: Northeast Foundation For Children, Inc.

Wooden, J. R., Jamison, S., Harper, P.L. & Cornelison, S. F. (2003) *Inch and miles: The journey to success.* Logan, Iowa: Perfection Learning Corporation.

Wooden, J., & Jamison, S. (1997). *Wooden: A Lifetime of Observations and Reflections On and Off the Court.* Chicago: Contemporary Books.

Zander, R. S., & Zander, B. (2000). *The Art of Possibility: Transforming professional and personal life.* New York: Penguin Books.

Gratitudes

It is with incredible gratitude that I offer the following acknowledg-
ments to so many people who have supported me on my journey!

The Founders of The Virtues Project, Linda Kavelin-Popov, Dr.
Dan Popov and John Kavelin for creating such a transformative proj-
ect and sharing it so generously with the world. Your love, guidance,
trust, support and patience empowered me to be the person I am today.
Barbara Swenson, for your willingness to come to Maryland to train
me as a Virtues Project facilitator and your generosity of time, spirit
and creativity in mentoring me to become a Master Facilitator. Yahzdi
Tillion, for your wisdom and guidance in encouraging me to focus on
the positive. Betsy Lydle Smith and Donna Wheatcroft, for introduc-
ing me to the field of character education and continuing to feed my
mind and spirit with inspiring and relevant resources and opportuni-
ties. Barbara Mackenzie, for starting me down the research path and
being my dedicated Virtues Project Facilitator Exchange co-facilitator.
Eva Marks MacIsaac for your incredible gift of discernment, wisdom
and leadership.

For all of my friends and colleagues in The Virtues Project global
community for inspiring me daily with ways you make the world a
better place. Tammy Jackson and Nancy Hanlin, for your assertive-
ness and enthusiasm, without your push I may not have ever had the
courage to offer a facilitator training. Dorrie Hancock, my dear Kiwi
friend, whose friendship, brilliance and enthusiasm for this work in-
spires me. Steve Snyder, our beloved Virtues Project webmaster, for
your unending diligence and generosity of service. Aria Gilchrist, for
your faithfulness, loyalty and generosity in sustaining the Virtues

Shop. Andrew Sherman, for your generosity of time, wisdom and legal counsel. Scott Feraco, for your creative vision, courage and sacrifice in creating The "V" Channel and your trust in bringing me in as your partner.

Laura Lippman, Kris Moore, Karen Walker, Lori Ann Delale O'Connor and Mary Terzian, from ChildTrends, for your faith, commitment and steadfast dedication in taking the lead on researching the project.

Lisa Glines, my soul sister, for your endless love and support on this journey of virtues. Kathy Johnson, for your generosity of time, tea and truthfulness and excellent editing. Becky Sipos, for your trust in bringing me into CEP and your journalistic encouragement. Marci Steiner, for your steadfast friendship and assistance in raising my vibration. Stacey Friedlander, for your loving guidance from the other side. Ellen MacDonald, for your lifetime of friendship, fun and editing excellence. Mark Sangimino, for your purity of spirit and commitment to always seeing the good in everyone. To Jenise Bobo, for your new friendship and your kind and supportive feedback. To my 12-Step brothers and sister in Alanon and Overeaters Anonymous for having the strength and courage to walk the path of happy destiny with me one day at a time.

Tamar Ruth, my assistant principal, and Kevin Payne, my principal, for your courage, insight and trust in creating a character development coaching position and hiring me as that coach. My friends and colleagues in Montgomery County Public Schools, MD, and especially my Greencastle Elementary School family for your courage, commitment and unity in transforming education. Pam Prue, my mentor throughout my professional career, whose gentle wisdom, guidance and discernment has moved me forward every step of the way since you interviewed me for my first teaching job in 1984. Jim DeGeorge, for your leadership, steadfast advocacy for children and unconditional support and guidance.

Incredible gratitude goes to all of the authors and teachers whose wisdom I have learned from and talked about in this book as well as all of the educators from around the world who so generously and lovingly contributed windows into their classrooms!

My sincere appreciation also goes to Steve Harrison and Geoffrey Berwind, of Bradley Communications, for your generosity of time and outstanding resources when helping me navigate the world of PR and marketing. Unending thanks goes to Joyce Wilde for your steadfast diligence and care doing the final edits. Gratitude goes to Nick Ippoliti and Brian Edmondson for your creativity and helpfulness in creating my website. To Justin Sachs and your team at Motivational Press for your patience and excellent support in publishing my book. To Ann McIndoo, my Author's Coach, and your team whose enthusiasm and excellence got this book out of my head and into your hands.

Finally, my heartfelt gratitude goes to my incredibly patient and supportive family for sharing this journey with me and to my loving Higher Power, whose guidance made this book and all things possible.

Gratitude

Gratitude is a constant attitude of thankfulness and appreciation for life as it unfolds. Living in the moment, we are open to abundance around us and within us. We express appreciation freely. We contemplate the richness of our life. We feast on beauty. We notice small graces and are thankful for daily gifts. In life's trials, we seek to understand, to accept, and to learn. Gratitude is the essence of genuine happiness. It is a virtue we can never have too much of. Gratitude is a continual celebration of life.

The Virtues Project™

The Virtues Project is a global grassroots initiative to inspire the practice of virtues in everyday life. The Project is sparking a global revolution of kindness, justice and integrity in more than 100 countries through its facilitators and Virtues Connections. It was honored by the United Nations and endorsed by the Dalai Lama. It is Five Strategies for bringing out the best in ourselves and others.

www.virtuesproject.org

The "V" Channel is a social media channel designed to engage and inspire young people to reach for a higher level of personal development. Teaching the "What, Why and How" of virtues through creative and entertaining videos and blogs, The "V" Channel provides useful and relevant lessons that can be applied in life regardless of one's cultural background and upbringing.

www.thevchannel.com

About Dara

An award-winning educator and inspiring speaker, Dara's life-long goal is to transform our schools and the systems that support them into environments that embrace the love of learning with the recognition of self-worth.

Dara is Chair of the Board and a Master Facilitator for the Virtues Project International Association, where she creates and delivers personal, professional and organizational development around the world, inspiring INDIVIDUALS to live more authentic, joyful lives, FAMILIES to raise children of compassion and integrity, EDUCATORS to create safe, caring and high performing learning communities and LEADERS to inspire excellence and ethics in the workplace. She is also an expert consultant to the Character Education Partnership in Washington, DC and Director of Education for The "V" Channel.

A National Board Certified Teacher, Dara was honored as Disney's 2005 Outstanding Elementary Teacher of the Year and Educator of the Year for the National Association for Self Esteem in 2009. After 16 years as a classroom teacher, five years as technology specialist for Montgomery County Public Schools in Maryland, and two years as an instructional coach in DC Public Schools, Dara receives requests from organizations around the world to facilitate meaningful workshops and retreats, provide hands on coaching and consulting and present inspiring keynotes.

Dara is happily married to Dave, who is committed to creating a more sustainable world through his work with The Livability Project. She is blessed with two grown caring and compassionate children, Dani and Jake, who are making their own dent in the universe in inspiring ways.

Dara invites you to connect with her:
Email: dara@darafeldman.com
Twitter @ Heart_of_Ed
Website: www.darafeldman.com

CPSIA information can be obtained at www.ICGtesting.com
Printed in the USA
BVOW01s1545090315

390854BV00003B/5/P